Anonymous

Alaska, and missions on the north Pacific coast

Anonymous

Alaska, and missions on the north Pacific coast

ISBN/EAN: 9783337817800

Printed in Europe, USA, Canada, Australia, Japan

Cover: Foto ©ninafisch / pixelio.de

More available books at **www.hansebooks.com**

ALASKA,

AND

MISSIONS ON THE NORTH PACIFIC COAST.

BY

Rev. SHELDON JACKSON, D.D.

FULLY ILLUSTRATED.

NEW YORK:
DODD, MEAD & COMPANY,
PUBLISHERS.

PREFACE.

IN the preparation of this volume, I have received valuable assistance from Wm. H. Dall, Esq., Smithsonian Institution; Mr. Marcus Baker, U. S. Coast Survey; Prof. J. W. Powell, Bureau of Ethnology, Smithsonian Institution; Prof. J. E. Nourse, U. S. Navy; Rev. John L. French, Washington; Hon. Wm. Gouverneur Morris, U. S. Treasury Agent; Messrs. Lee & Shepard, Boston; Mr. Ivan Petroff, San Francisco, and Mr. E. Conklin, New York City, to all of whom I return thanks.

THE AUTHOR.

DENVER, COL., February 2d, 1880.

CONTENTS.

CHAPTER I.
                                                                PAGE
Great Extent of Country—Natural Phenomena—Divisions—
Agriculture—Islands—Mountains—Volcanoes—Glaciers
—Aurora Borealis—Mineral Springs—Rivers—Furs—
Fisheries—Lumber—Coal—Petroleum—Copper—Iron—
Sulphur—Gold—Climate—Kuro-Siwo—Routes of Travel. 13

CHAPTER II.
Population—Customs—Houses—Dances—Feasts—Cremation—Religious Beliefs—Shamanism................... 62

CHAPTER III.
The Degradation of Indian Women in Alaska—Female Infanticide—The Sale of Girls—Female Slavery—Polygamy
—Habitations of Cruelty—Widow-burning—Murder of
the Old and Feeble................................. 115

CHAPTER IV.
Greek and Lutheran Churches — Preliminary Steps Toward
American Missions.................................. 124

CHAPTER V.
The Commencement of Presbyterian Missions in Alaska—
Mrs. A. R. McFarland—Her Varied Duties—Sickness and
Death of Clah—Christmas Welcome 140

CONTENTS.

CHAPTER VI.

Indian Constitutional Convention—Great Speech of Toy-a-att—Native Police—Indians making a Treaty of Peace—Need of a Home for Girls—Witchcraft—Home Commenced—Arrival of Rev. S. Hall Young...................... 166

CHAPTER VII.

Sketch of Sitka—Arrival of Rev. John G. Brady and Miss Fannie E. Kellogg—Commencement of School—Missionary Journeys of Mr. Brady—Marriage of Miss Kellogg—School of Mr. Alonzo E. Austin........................ 196

CHAPTER VIII.

Appeal for Funds for Mission Buildings—The Response—Joy at the Mission—Arrival of Dr. Corlies and Family—Coming of the Roman Catholics—Arrival of Miss Maggie J. Dunbar as Teacher—Visit of Rev. Henry Kendall, D.D., and others—Rejoicing of the Indians—Organization of the Church—Erection of Buildings.................. 216

CHAPTER IX.

A Canoe Voyage—Deserted Indian Village—Toiling in Rowing—Councils with Chilcats, Hydas, and Tongas—New Fields—Fort Tongas—Driving before the Storm—An Indian Welcome.................................. 254

CHAPTER X.

Missions of the Church Missionary Society of England in British Columbia on the Border of Alaska—Cannibalism—A Christian Village—Triumphs of Grace—Tradition Concerning the First Appearance of the Whites......... 273

CHAPTER XI.

Missions of the Methodist Church of Canada in British Columbia—A Great Revival—Wonderful Experiences.... 302

ILLUSTRATIONS

	PAGE.
Portrait of the author, steel engraving (Frontispiece).	
Map of Alaska.	
Travelling on a dog sled	16
Eskimo village	17
Ptarmigan	19
An Arctic mountain scene	20
Capturing a whale in Behring Sea	21
Alaska House	27
Sled dog	30
Eskimo sled	32
Snow shovel	32
Stone kettle	35
Bone lamp	35
Bone fork	35
Aurora borealis	39
Breaking up of the ice in the Yukon	43
Fishing village	47
Hunting walrus	55
Walrus head	57
Knife for cutting blocks of snow	59
Seal-skin canoe	59
Innuit arrows	59
Innuit knife and saw	59
Eskimo head	61
Playing the Key-low-tik	63
Key-low-tik and Ken-toon	65

ILLUSTRATIONS.

	PAGE.
Eskimo snow house	68
Diagram of the same	69
Eskimo hunter	70
Eskimo woman	71
Bone comb	72
Horns of musk ox	77
Hunting musk ox	75
Carved images, Fort Wrangell	81
Totem poles, Fort Wrangell	79
Ladle from horns of musk ox	84
Ivory knives, forks, and spoons	85
Carved ivory comb	85
Deer-skin boots	86
Carved canoe-head	86
Tomb of a chief's son, Fort Wrangell	88
Innuit grave	89
Ingalik grave	89
Ekogmut grave	90
Cremation	93
Innuit knife	99
Stone knife	99
Carved spoon-handle	99
Aleutian mask	100
Innuit bone charm	101
Seal-tooth head-dress	105
Innuit harpoon heads	106
Shaman and sick man	111
Tattooing	119
Eskimo woman and babe	123
Sitka	125
Chief's house, Fort Wrangell	134
Fort Wrangell village	141
Mrs. A. R. McFarland	146
The McFarland school	149
Clah	159
Alaska Fox	165
Shaaks lying in state	179

ILLUSTRATIONS.

	PAGE.
The Home, Fort Wrangell	187
Rev. S. Hall Young	191
A Puffin	195
Rear view of Greek church, Sitka	197
Bay of Sitka	199
The Castle and Custom-House, Sitka	201
Rev. John G. Brady	203
The barracks, Sitka	207
Mission group, Fort Wrangell	231
Seal-skin shoes	241
Seal Skin moccasins	241
Indians gambling	243
A scalp dance	257
Stone implements	262
Aurora on the Yukon	267
Alaska sea-gull	272
Dog eaters	277
Kindling a fire by friction	285
Indian family on the Yukon	291
A canoe voyage	301
Great medicine man	303
Methodist Church, Fort Simpson	309
Heathen dance, Alaska	313
Sled	327

INNUIT NEEDLE-CASE.

CHAPTER I.

Great Extent of Country—Natural Phenomena—Divisions —Agriculture—Islands—Mountains—Volcanoes— Glaciers — Aurora Borealis—Mineral Springs—Rivers—Furs—Fisheries— Lumber —Coal—Petroleum—Copper—Iron—Sulphur— Gold — Climate —Kuro-Siwo—Routes of Travel.

> " Go ye and look upon that land,
> That far, vast land that few behold ;
> Go journey with the seasons through
> Its wastes, and learn how limitless."

DURING the spring of 1867 the United States Senate was the scene of a stormy debate over the ratification of the treaty with Russia for the purchase of Alaska. Upon that occasion Charles Sumner delivered one of his finest orations. As he unfolded the resources of that vast, distant, and unknown land, even learned men listened with eager interest. As he presented its intimate relations to our Pacific coast possessions, patriotism glowed with a warmer enthusiasm. As he spoke of its grand future, every heart was thrilled, and the determined opposition of many was overcome.

The treaty, which was made March 30th, 1867, was ratified by the United States Senate on the 28th of May; and on the 18th of October, 1867, Russian America was formally turned over to the United States upon the payment of $7,200,000.

The attention and interest that had been awakened at the time of the heated debate in the Senate soon died away. The American people almost lost sight of their new possession, or only occasionally recalled it as Secretary Seward's folly.

This was not unexpected to that great statesman. Nor did it shake his confidence in the value of that country. At a public dinner given him upon retiring to private life, to the question, "Mr. Seward, what do you consider the most important act of your official life?" he unhesitatingly replied, "The purchase of Alaska;" then, after a moment's pause, he added, "But it may take two generations before the purchase is appreciated."

The old statesman was right. It was his crowning glory to have added a new empire to his country's domain. For, as its name signifies, it is an empire of itself.

Alaska is an English corruption of the native word "Al-ak-shak," which means "a great country or continent."

And it is indeed a great country, covering over 580,107 square miles, an area equal to the original thirteen States of the Union with the great "Northwest Territory" added; or, in other words, Alaska is as large as all of the United States east of the Mississippi River and north of Alabama, Georgia, and

North Carolina. Its extreme breadth from east to west is two thousand two hundred miles in an air line. According to Professor Guyot, a recognized authority on all geographical matters, the island of Attu in Alaska is as far west of San Francisco as the coast of Maine is east of that city ; or, in other words, San Francisco is the great middle city between the extreme east and west of the United States. The extreme breadth of Alaska from north to south is one thousand four hundred miles. The shore line up and down the bays and around the islands, according to the United States Coast Survey, measures twenty-five thousand miles, or two and one half times more than the Atlantic and Pacific coast lines of the remaining portion of the United States. The coast of Alaska, if extended in a straight line, would belt the globe.

Commencing at the north shore of Dixon Inlet, in latitude 54' 40', the coast sweeps in a long regular curve north and west to the entrance of Prince William's Sound, a distance of 550 miles ; thence 725 miles south and west to Unimak Pass at the end of the Aliaska Peninsula. From this pass the Aleutian chain of islands sweep 1075 miles in a long curve almost across to Asia, the dividing line between Asia and Alaska being, according to the treaty made with Russia, the meridian of 193° west longitude. North of Unimak Pass the coast forms a zigzag line to Point Barrow on the Arctic Ocean. The general shape of Alaska is that of the head and horns of an ox inverted ; the main body of land forming the head, the Peninsula and Aleutian Islands the one horn, and the South-eastern Peninsula the other.

This physical configuration naturally divides it into three districts—the Yukon, extending from the Alaskan range of mountains to the Arctic Ocean ; the Aleutian, embracing the Aliaska Peninsula and islands west of the 155th degree of longitude, and the Sitkan, including South-eastern Alaska.

TRAVELLING ON DOG-SLED.

Concerning the Yukon District but little is known, except of the coast and along the Yukon River. "The Coast Pilot," a publication of the United States Coast Survey, represents the country between Norton Sound and the Arctic Ocean as "a vast moorland, whose level is only interrupted by promontories and isolated mountains, with numerous lakes, bogs, and peat-beds. Wherever drainage exists, the

ESKIMO VILLAGE, ALASKA.

VEGETATION IN ALASKA.

ground is covered with a luxuriant herbage and produces the rarest as well as most beautiful plants. The aspect of some of these spots is very gay. Many flowers are large, their colors bright, and though white and yellow predominate, other tints are not uncommon. Summer sets in most rapidly in May,

ALASKA PTARMIGAN.

and the landscape is quickly overspread with a lively green." The extreme heat and constant sunshine cause it to produce rank vegetation. The commercial value of this section is mainly in its furs.

Turnips, radishes, and salad have been successfully raised at St. Michael, Nulato, and Fort Yukon. Grasses and fodder are abundant ; among the former are the Kentucky blue-grass, wood-meadow and blue-joint grasses. This latter averages three feet in height. The red and black currants, gooseberries, cranberries, raspberries, thimbleberries, salmonberries, blueberries, killikinik berries, bearberries, dewberries, twinberries, service or heath berries, mossberries, and roseberries, grow in great abundance in all sections of Alaska. Hundreds of barrels

AN ARCTIC MOUNTAIN SCENE.

of wild cranberries are annually picked by the Indians and shipped to San Francisco.

The Aleutian District is largely mountainous and of volcanic formation. Between the mountains and the sea are, however, many natural prairies, with a rich soil of vegetable mould and clay, and covered with perennial wild grasses.

CAPTURING A WHALE IN BERING'S SEA.

Dr. Kellogg, botanist of the United States Exploring Expedition, writes : "Unalaska abounds in grasses, with a climate better adapted for haying than the coast of Oregon. The cattle were remarkably fat. Milk is abundant."

William H. Dall, of the Smithsonian Institution, predicts that the Aleutian District will yet furnish California with its best butter and cheese.

This district, except at the eastern end, is without timber larger than a shrub. The principal resource at present is in the wonderful fisheries off its coast.

The Sitkan District is mountainous in the extreme, and the larger portion covered with dense forests. The great wealth of this district is in its lumber, fish, and minerals. Many garden vegetables are raised with success. Rev. John G. Brady, Presbyterian missionary at Sitka, writes :

"The Kake Indians furnished the Russians with potatoes. Some of the natives at Wrangell are clearing off garden patches this year. Much can be done in this direction, for Alaska will furnish vegetables for a teeming population. There are several thousand acres in the neighborhood of this place, upon which the finest vegetables may be raised with certainty. The soil, for the most part, is a vegetable mould mixed with sand. Mr. Smiegh, of this place, has had a garden for the last seven years. He says that he has grown cabbages weighing twenty-seven pounds. He has tried peas, carrots, leeks, parsnips, turnips, lettuce, radishes, onions, potatoes, celery, parsley, horseradish and rhubarb. He has tried cucumbers and beans, but they did not do well. Cauliflower and celery surpass any that he has raised in other places. The wild black currants abound in the woods. The tame currants do well, and are sure. Gooseberries do well, and have a delicate flavor. The cabbage grows wild, and six or eight inches in diameter. Mr. Burns, who has had a garden for the last three years, agrees with Mr. Smiegh. The strawberry grows wild near Mount Edgecumbe."

During the summer of 1879 I cut at Fort Wrangell wild timothy that would average five feet in height, and blue-grass that would average six feet, the longest stem measured seven feet three inches. Professor Muir, State Geologist of California, testifies that he never met anywhere outside of the tropics such rank vegetation as in this district.

Alaska is not only "a great land" in its large area, but also in its natural phenomena. Captain Butler, an English officer, crossing that great "north-land," writes that "Nature has here graven her image in such colossal characters that man seems to move slowly amid an ocean frozen rigid by the lapse of time—frozen into those things we call mountains, rivers, prairies, and forests. Rivers whose single lengths roll through twice two thousand miles of shore line; prairies over which a traveller can steer for weeks without resting his gaze on aught save the dim verge of the ever-shifting horizon; mountains rent by rivers, ice-topped, glacier-seared, impassable; forests whose sombre pines darken a region half as large as Europe. In summer a land of sound, a land echoing with the voices of birds, the ripple of running water, the mournful music of the waving

ISLANDS.

pine branch. In winter a land of silence, its great rivers glimmering in the moonlight, wrapped in their shrouds of ice ; its still forests rising weird and spectral against the aurora-lighted horizon ; its nights so still that the moving streamers across the northern skies seem to carry to the ear a sense of sound."

Alaska is the great island region of the United States, having off its southern coast an archipelago rivalling the better known archipelagoes of the Southern Pacific. The 732 miles of latitude from the western terminus of the Northern Pacific Railroad, at the head of Puget Sound in Washington Territory to the head of Lynn Channel in Alaska contain one of the most remarkable stretches of inland ocean navigation in the world. It is remarkable for its bold shores, deep water, numerous channels, innumerable bays and harbors, abundance of fuel and fresh water, and shelter from the swells of the ocean. The great mountainous islands of Vancouver, Queen Charlotte, Prince of Wales, Wrangell, Baranoff, Chichagoff, and others form a complete breakwater, so that the traveller can enjoy an ocean voyage of a thousand miles without getting out to sea and without seasickness, the trip being made through channels between the islands and the main land.

The labyrinth of channels around and between the islands that are in some places less than a quarter of a mile wide, and yet too deep to drop anchor, the mountains rising from the water's edge from 1000 to 8000 feet, and covered with dense forests of evergreen far up into the snow that crowns their summits ; the frequent track of the avalanche, cutting a broad road from mountain-top to water's edge; the beautiful cascades born of glaciers or the overflow of high inland lakes, pouring over mountain precipices or gliding like a silver ribbon down their sides; the deep gloomy sea-fiords, cleaving the mountains far into the interior; the beautiful kaleidoscopic vistas opening up among the innumerable islets; mountain-tops domed, peaked, and sculptured by glaciers; the glaciers themselves sparkling and glistening in the sunlight, dropping down from the mountain heights like some great swollen river, filled with drift-wood and ice, and suddenly arrested in its flow—all go to make up a scene of grandeur and beauty that cannot be placed upon canvas or adequately described with words. When the attractions of that trip are better known, thousands will make a pleasure tour along the coast of Alaska.

The southern portion of this great archipelago is in Washington Territory, the central portion in British Columbia, and the northern portion in Alaska. This latter has been named the Alexander Archipelago, in honor of the Czar of Russia. It is about 300 miles north and south and 75 miles east and west, containing 1100 islands that have been counted. The aggregate area of these islands is 14,142 square miles. Six hundred miles to the westward is the Kadiak group, aggregating 5676 square miles, then the Shumagin group, containing 1031 square miles, and the Aleutian chain, with an area of 6391 square miles. To the northward is the Pribyloff (seal islands) group, containing, with the other islands in Bering's Sea, 3963 square miles. The total area of the islands of

AN ALASKA HOUSE OF CEDAR PLANK.

Alaska is 31,205 square miles, which would make a State as large as the great State of Maine.

It is the region of the highest mountain-peaks in the United States. The coast range of California and the Rocky Mountain range of Colorado and Montana unite in Alaska to form the Alaskan Mountains. This range, instead of continuing northward, to the Arctic Ocean, as the old atlases represent, turns to the south-westward, extends through and forms the Aliaska Peninsula, and then gradually sinks into the Pacific Ocean, leaving only the highest peaks visible above the water. These peaks form the Aleutian chain of islands. These islands decrease in size, height, and frequency as the mountain range sinks lower into the ocean. Unimak, the most eastern of the chain, has that magnificent volcano Shishaldin, 9000 feet high; then Unalashka, 5691 feet; next Atka, 4852 feet; then Kyska, 3700 feet, and Attu, the most western of the group, only 3084 feet high.

In the Alaskan range are the highest peaks in the United States—Mount St. Elias, 19,500 feet high; Mount Cook, 16,000 feet; Mount Crillon, 15,900; Mount Fairweather, 15,500, and numerous others. In addition to the Alaskan range, the Shaktolik and Ulukuk Hills, near Norton Sound; the Yukon and Romanzoff Hills, north of the Yukon River; the Kaiyuh and Nowikakat Mountains, east and south of the river, and a low range of hills bordering the Arctic coast.

Alaska contains the great volcanic system of the United States. Grewingk enumerates 61 volcanoes, mainly on the Aliaska Peninsula and Aleutian Islands, that have been active since the settlement by Europeans. The violence of the volcanic forces is said to be decreasing, so that only ten are now belching out smoke and ashes.

One of the extinct volcanoes is Mount Edgecumbe, near Sitka. Its funnel-shaped crater is 2000 feet

SLED-DOG.

across and about 400 feet deep. It is on the southern point of Kruzoff Island, and has an elevation of 2855 feet.

Rev. John G. Brady gives the following traditions concerning it: "This is a Mount Olympus for the natives. They say that the first Indian pair lived peaceably for a long time, and were blessed with children. But one day a family jar occurred. The husband and wife grew very angry at each other. For this the man was changed into a wolf and the woman into a raven. The metamorphosed woman flew down into the open crater of Mount Edgecumbe, lit on a stump, and is now holding the earth on her wings. Whenever there is thunder and lightning around the summit, it is only the wolf giving vent to his rage while he is trying to pull her off the stump. It would be a great calamity if she should lose her grip, for then the earth would be upset and all who live upon it perish. So whenever it thunders the Indians take stones and pound on the floors of their houses to encourage the raven to hold to the stump.

"Another myth is that a being who is half dog and half Indian lives on the top. He comes down once a year near the harbor to catch halibut. He covers himself with an eagle's skin. But upon his first attempts to fly to the crest he failed. In his efforts he scratched the grooves and deep gullies in the mountain-side. After repeated attempts he got so that he could fly, and now he feeds on whales, which he carries to his home in the crater."

On the Naass River, just across from Southern Alaska, is a remakable lava overflow from a volcano in the neighborhood. The Indian tale is that some cruel children, playing at the mouth of a small stream, were catching the salmon, and, cutting open their backs, put stones in them and let them go again. The Good Spirit, being angry, set the river on fire and burnt up the children, and the Lava Plain remains as the memento. The diverted channel of

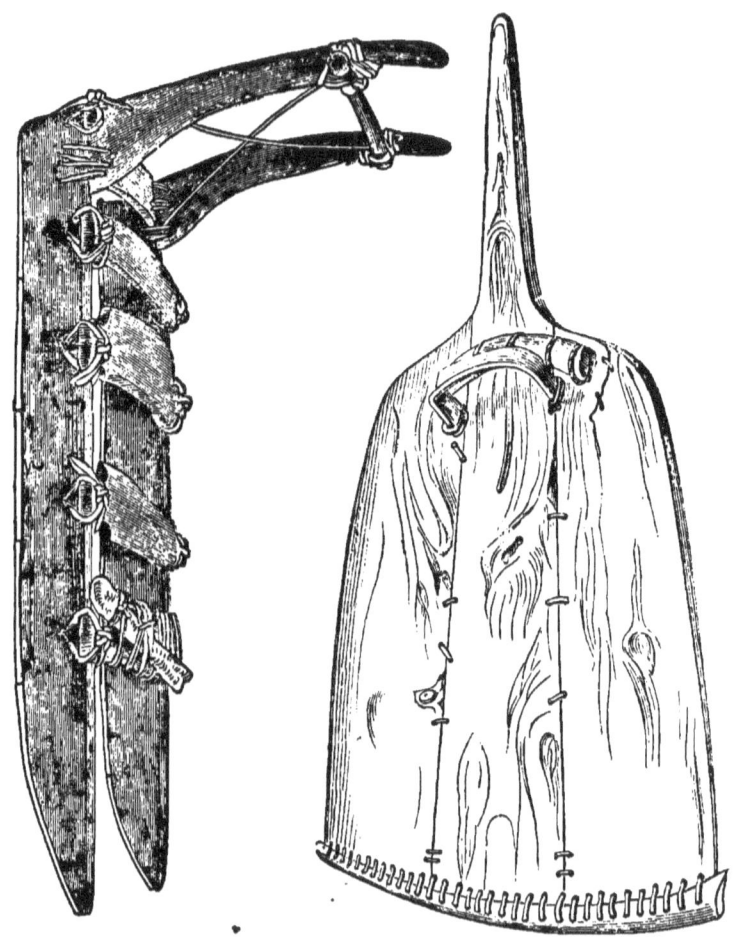

ESKIMO SLED AND SNOW-SHOVEL.

the Naass River is still called New River by the Indians.

GLACIERS. 33

A correspondent of the San Francisco *Bulletin* speaks of a fresh eruption in 1878 on the Island of Umnak : " The inhabitants of villages on the west and south side of Unalashka Island complain of the sudden disappearance of fish from their shores and streams. The cause of the disastrous phenomenon is a volcanic eruption on the adjoining island of Umnak, accompanied by a heavy fall of hot ashes and earthquakes. The volcano on Umnak has been considered extinct for many years past, but two weeks ago a new crater opened, at least ten miles away on a sloping plain of but slight elevation above the sea level. Owing to the latter circumstance the lava flows but slowly, and hardens before it reaches the shore, but the fall of ashes extends over a large area of land and water. Persons passing the east side of the island in canoes suffer from sulphurous gases whenever the wind blows from the shore, and the thundering noise of the eruption can be heard at the village of Unalashka during the still hours of the night."

It is the great glacier region. From Bute Inlet to Unimak Pass nearly every deep gulch has its glacier, some of which are vastly greater and grander than any glacier of the Alps.

On Lynn Channel is a glacier computed to be 1200 feet thick at the " snout" or lower projection. In one of the gulches of Mount Fairweather is a glacier that extends fifty miles to the sea, where it ends abruptly in a perpendicular ice-wall 300 feet high and eight miles broad. Thirty-five miles above Wrangell, on the Stickeen River, between two mountains 3000 feet high, is an immense glacier forty miles long and at the base four to five miles across, and variously estimated from 500 to 1000 feet high or deep.

Opposite this glacier, just across the river, are large boiling springs. The Indians regard this glasier as a personification of a mighty ice-god, who has issued from his mountain home invested with power before which all nature bows in submission. They describe him as crashing his way through the cañon till its glistening pinnacles looked upon the domains of the river-god, and that after a conflict the ice-god conquered, and spanned the river's breadth so completely that the river-god was forced to crawl underneath. The Indians then sent their medicine-man to learn how this could be avoided. The answer came that if a noble chief and fair maiden would offer themselves a sacrifice by taking passage under the long, dark, winding ice-arch, his anger would be appeased, and the river be allowed to go on its way undisturbed. When the two were found and adorned, their arms bound, and seated in a canoe, the fatal journey was made, and the ice has never again attempted to cross the river. At one of these glaciers ships from California have anchored and taken on cargoes of ice.

Another tradition given me by one of their medicine-men was that years ago a tribe which resided on the upper waters of the Stickeen River wanted to come down and see the great salt water. But the great ice-mountain of the Stickeen at that time spanned the river and barricaded all passing up or down. The water, indeed, ran under the ice, but they did not know whether they could go through safely with their canoes. While they were assembled in solemn council, consulting about it, two old men

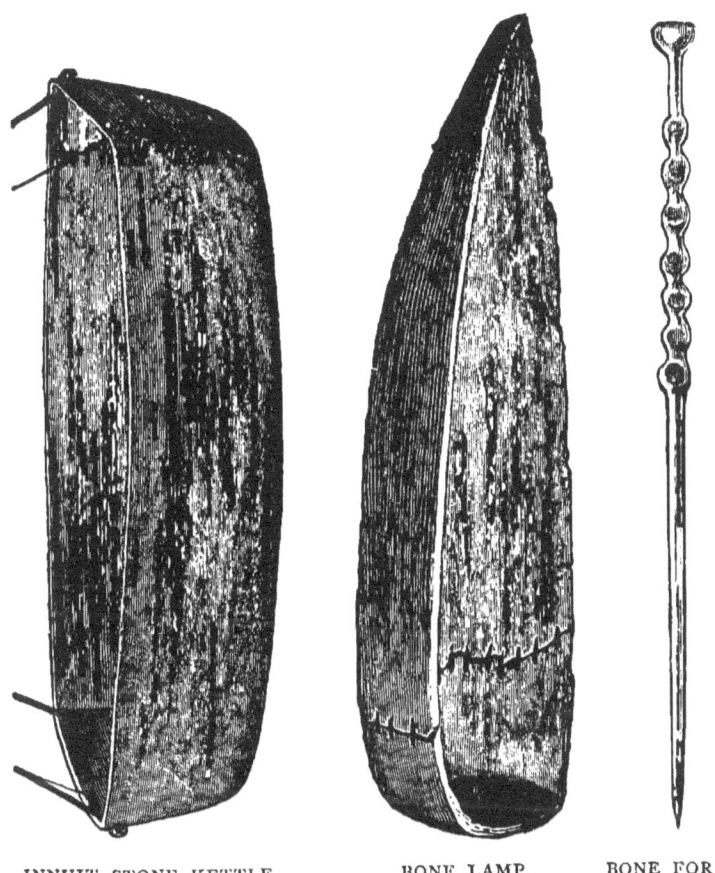

INNUIT STONE KETTLE.   BONE LAMP.   BONE FORK.

of the tribe offered to attempt the passage. They said : " If we are lost, it will only shorten our lives a very little ; but if we succeed, then you can all folow." They chanted their death-song and disappeared beneath the ice. The passage was made safely, and their people followed.

Professor John Muir, State Geologist of California, accompanying our party on a trip to a large glacier near Cape Fanshaw, thus describes it :

"The whole front and brow of this majestic glacier is dashed and sculptured into a maze of yawning chasms and crevices and a bewildering variety of strange architectural forms, appalling to the strongest nerves, but novel and beautiful beyond measure—clusters of glittering lance-tipped spires, gables and obelisks, bold outstanding bastions and plain mural cliffs, adorned along the top with fretted cornice and battlement, while every gorge and crevasse, chasm and hollow was filled with light, shimmering and pulsing in pale blue tones of ineffable tenderness and loveliness. The day was warm, and back on the broad waving bosom of the glacier water-streams were outspread in a complicated network, each in its own frictionless channel cut down through the porous, decaying ice of the surface into the quick and living blue, and flowing with a grace of motion and a ring and gurgle and flashing of light to be found only on the crystal hills and dales of a glacier.

"Along the sides we could see the mighty flood grinding against the granite with tremendous pressure, rounding the outswelling bosses, deepening and smoothing the retreating hollows, and shaping every portion of the mountain walls into the forms they were meant to have, when in the fulness of appointed time the ice-tool should be lifted and set aside by the sun. Every feature glowed with intention, reflecting the earth-plans of God. Back two or three miles from the front the current is now probably about twelve hundred feet deep ; but when we examine the walls, the grooved and rounded features, so surely glacial, show that in the earlier days of the ice-age they were all overswept, this glacier having flowed at a height of from three to four thousand feet above its present level."

Dall, in his "Alaska and its Resources," says : " Any account of Alaska would be incomplete which did not include a mention of the remarkable hot and mineral springs which are so numerous." There are large ones south of Sitka, also on Perenosna Bay, on Amagat Island, and Port Moller. On Unimak Island is a lake of sulphur. Near the volcano Pogrumnoi are hot marshes. Boiling springs are found on the Islands Akhun, Atka, Unimak, Adakh, Sitignak, and Kanaga. These latter have for ages been used by the natives for cooking food. In the crater of Goreloi is a vast boiling, steaming mineral spring eighteen miles in circumference. A lake strongly impregnated with nitre is found on Beaver Island. The thermal springs on the Island of Unalashka hold sulphur in solution. Noises proceed from them occasionally like the booming of a cannon. The natives have a tradition that long ago the volcanoes in this neighborhood fought with each other and Makushin came off victor.

The northern portion of Alaska, within the Arctic Circle, is famous for its beautiful auroral displays. Bancroft describes them "as flashing out in prismatic coruscations, throwing a brilliant arch from east to west—now in variegated oscillations, graduating through all the various tints of blue and green and violet and crimson, darting, flashing, or streaming in yellow columns upward, downward; now blazing steadily, now in wavy undulations, sometimes up to the very zenith; momentarily lighting up the surrounding scenery, but only to fall back into darkness." Whymper speaks of one display seen on the Yukon as representing a vast undulating snake crossing the heavens. The superstitious natives, that see in all phenomena evidence of the spirits they fear, consider these displays as the reflection of the lights used by the spirits in their dances in their northern homes. "Singularly enough," says Dall, "they call the constellation of Ursa Major by the name of Okil-Ok'puk, and consider him to be ever on the watch while the other spirits carry on their festivities. None of the spirits are regarded as supreme, nor have the Innuit tribes any idea of a deity, a state of future reward and punishment, or any system of morality."

Alaska contains not only one of the largest rivers of the United States, but also of the world.

The river Yukon is 70 miles wide across its five mouths and intervening deltas. At some points along its lower course one bank cannot be seen from the other. For the first thousand miles it is from one to five miles wide, and in some places, including islands, it is twenty miles from main bank to main bank. Navigable for 1500 miles, it is computed to be 2000 miles long. Upon its upper waters, within

AURORA BOREALIS.

the Arctic Circle, is Fort Yukon, a post of the Hudson Bay Company. At this far distant post, where tidings from the outside world only reach once a year, is a Scotch missionary. The British Church looks well after its own people. On its banks live thousands who know neither its outlet nor its source, and yet, recognizing its greatness, proudly call themselves the "Men of Yukon."

The other principal rivers of the Territory are the Stickeen, 250 miles long ; the Chilcat, the Copper, the Fire, the Nushergak, a large shallow stream 150 miles long ; the Kuskoquim, next to the Yukon in size, and between 500 and 600 miles long ; the Tananah, 250 miles. This river is half a mile wide at its mouth, with a very strong current ; the Nowikakat, 112 miles, and the Porcupine. The latter three are tributaries of the Yukon. The only river of any size flowing into the Arctic Ocean is the Colville, for a long time supposed to be the outlet of the Yukon.

The chief value of Alaska to Russia was its wonderful fur supplies. And when the Territory was sold to the United States the most prominent attraction was the seal-fur fisheries on the Pribyloff group of islands in Bering's Sea. To protect these valuable interests the Government leased these islands for twenty years to an incorporated company known as the "Alaska Commercial Company." They pay the Government an annual rental of $55,000 for the islands, and a royalty of $262,500 a year on the 100,000 seal-skins allowed by law to be taken.

Thus these two little islands—St. Paul, 13 miles long and 6 wide, and St. George, 10 miles long and

6 wide—furnish nearly all the seal-skins used in the markets of the world, and have paid a revenue into the United States Treasury from 1871 to 1880 of over two and one half million dollars; and yet it is thought by some that Alaska was a worthless purchase.

The Alaska Company has thirty-five trading stations in addition to its seal-fisheries.

The next most valuable fur is that of the sea-otter, of which about $100,000 worth are annually taken. Formerly these skins were worth from $200 to $500 each in gold; in 1880 they are quoted at from $20 to $200 each.

The principal land fur-bearing animals are the several varieties of the fox, the mink, beaver, marten, lynx, otter, black bear, and wolverine. There are also the skins of the whistler, reindeer, mountain goat and sheep, ermine, marmot, muskrat, and wolf. The fur product amounts to $1,000,000 annually.

Alaska is also a great fish region. All the early navigators and explorers, from Cook to the present time, have spoken of its immense numbers of salmon, cod, herring, halibut, mullet, ulicon, etc. There are no other such fisheries in the known world. A missionary thus describes a fishing scene on the Naass River: "I went up to their fishing-ground on the Naass River, where some five thousand Indians had assembled. It was what is called their 'small fishing.' The salmon catch is at another time. These small fish form a valuable article for food, and also for oil. They come up for six weeks only, and with great regularity. The Naass, where I visited it, was about a

BREAKING UP OF THE ICE ON THE YUKON RIVER.

mile and a half wide, and the fish had come up in great quantities, so great that with three nails upon a stick an Indian would rake in a canoe full in a short time. Five thousand Indians were gathered together from British Columbia and Alaska, decked out in their strange and fantastic costumes. Their faces were painted red and black, feathers on their heads, and imitations of wild beasts on their dresses. Over the fish was an immense cloud of sea-gulls—so many and so thick that, as they hovered about looking for fish, the sight resembled a heavy fall of snow. Over the gulls were eagles soaring about watching their chance. After the small fish had come up larger fish from the ocean There was the halibut, the cod, the porpoise, and the fin-back whale. Man life, fish life, and bird life—all under intense excitement. And all that animated life was to the heathen people a life of spirits. They paid court to and worshipped the fish they were to assist in destroying, greeting them, 'You fish! you fish! You are all chiefs, you are.'"

Cod are found from the Seal Islands southward, but are most abundant on the banks in the Kadiak and Aleutian archipelagoes. Three San Franciso firms engaged in the business caught 3000 tons during 1879 on the banks off the Shumagin Islands.

Alaska can also supply the world with salmon, herring, and halibut of the best quality. Salmon canneries have been established near Sitka, at Klawak, and at Kasa-an Bay. As many as 7000 salmon have been taken at one haul of the seine. Salmon are frequently caught in Cook's Inlet weighing 60 pounds each, and exceptional ones 120 pounds each.

Alaska is the great reserve lumber region of the United States. It is only a question of a few years when the forests of Maine, Michigan, Wisconsin, Minnesota, and even Puget Sound, will be denuded of their best timber. Then the country will appreciate those thousands of square miles of yellow cedar, white spruce, hemlock, and balsam fir that densely cover the south-eastern section of Alaska. The Hon. William H. Seward, upon returning from a trip to Alaska, said, in a public address, "I venture to predict that the North Pacific coast will become a common ship-yard for the American Continent, and speedily for the whole world. Europe, Asia, Africa, and even the Atlantic American States have either exhausted or are exhausting their native supplies of timber and lumber. Their last and only resort must be to the North Pacific."

The indications are that Alaska is very rich in minerals. It should be remembered that there has been no scientific or geological survey of Alaska; that the long Russian occupation sought only the development of the fur interests, and that the minerals which have been found in the country have not been developed sufficiently to determine their full economic value.

Ex-Mayor Dodge, of Sitka, writes: "From the earliest history of the country to the present day the existence of gold, silver, copper, iron, marble, and coal has been constantly attested. We have the undeniable authority of eminent scientific officials

AN ALASKA FISHING VILLAGE.

and the statements of strangers temporarily visiting the coast."

Coal is found all along the coast. The most valuable of the known deposits is found in Cook's Inlet. It is of excellent quality for the use of steamships The quantity seems to be unlimited.

Petroleum is found floating on a lake near the Bay of Katmai. It is quite odorless, and in its crude state has been used by the Russians for lubricating machinery. Large deposits have also been found on Copper River.

Specimens of pure copper have been found in many places. It is so abundant on Copper River as to give the name to the stream. At Kasa-an Bay a valuable mine of bronze copper is being worked by an English company. Lead in small quantities is found on Whale Bay, south of Sitka, and also in Kadiak Island.

Iron is common to many sections of the Territory. Graphite is found at several places. A fine quality of marble exists in inexhaustible quantities. A fine quality of bismuth is found on Vostovia Mountain. Kaolin fire-clay, and gypsum are also found. Sulphur exists in large quantities. Amethysts, zeolites, garnets, agates, carnelians, and fossil ivory are found. Indeed, the people of the United States have no conception of the mineral wealth of Alaska.

Gold is found in a number of places, and supposed to exist in many others. But little prospecting has been done on account of the hostility of the natives. Up the Stickeen River through Alaska, over on the head waters of Deese River, are the Cassiar mines of

British Columbia, where from 2500 to 3000 miners have spent several summers in placer mining with profit. The annual product of these mines is from $800,000 to $1,000,000. As the precious metals abound the whole length of the mountain chain in South and Central America, Mexico, Arizona, Colorado, Utah, Nevada, Montana, British America, and Cassiar (on the edge of Alaska), the presumption is that the precious deposits continue through Alaska.

Captain J. W. White, United States Revenue Marine, in his report to the Department, says:

"With regard to the resources of that portion of Alaska which we have visited, I would mention the recent discovery of gold on the several streams of the main land, between the parallels of $57° 10'$ and $58°$, emptying into Stephen's Passage, some thirty or forty white men and as many Indians being now engaged in mining there, making $5 to $10 a day. I saw at Sitka very rich specimens of gold-bearing quartz and silver ore which had been obtained from lodes on Baranoff (Sitka) Island."

The mines referred to on Stephen's Passage are called Shuck, and are about 75 miles north of Fort Wrangell. The only quartz mining at present is in the neighborhood of Sitka.

The *Alaska Appeal* of March 6th, 1879, gives the following review of the mines:

" From Sitka to the head of Silver Bay is ten miles over a beautiful sheet of water deep enough for vessels of any tonnage, which can lie at anchor twenty-five feet from the shore. From this point of the shore to the first mine, known as the Haley and Miletich mine, is less than one mile. The shaft on this ledge is down forty-five feet. The ledge is eight and one half feet wide, with two well-defined walls in slate formation, and the rock at that depth resembling that in the Stewart tunnel. Said tunnel is one quarter of a mile north-east, and crosses the same gulch on which the Haley and Miletich is situated, both running east and west and parallel with each other. The tunnel is in on the ledge 108 feet, and the shaft downward eighty-five feet from the surface in a ledge fourteen and one half feet wide. When first worked the ledge was only one foot in width, and kept widening as we penetrated the hill until it got so wide that we cut on one side of the vein, with a five and one half foot drift through the body of ore, the walls being also of slate formation. We ran a side-drift through the ore body, and struck the wall at some distance back from where the tunnel ends at present. The croppings of this ledge are visible for one mile, where they disappear in a dip.

"Next comes the Wicked Fall mine, the croppings of which are four and one half feet wide. A dark blue plumbago ore appears a some distance below the croppings.

"Next is the lode known as the Haley and Francis lode, not much improved, but prospects very well in gold and galena. It runs irregularly with reference to the other lodes, and is rich in free gold.

"The next is the Bald Mountain lode, having the same east and west course, and prospects very well in gold and galena, and has, like the last-mentioned mine, a slate formation.

"Next is the Lake Mountain lode, which prospects well in free gold. Much of it is black sulphurets, and the ledge runs in a slate formation.

"Next is the Witch Mine, very rich in gold. The ledge is broken up and decomposed. The range is east and west. The ledge runs in a slate formation, and is from six to seven feet wide. There is an abundance of rotten granite in the vicinity of the lode.

"Next is the Last Chance mine, a very extensive ledge of ribbon quartz—such as is well known to California miners—in a slate formation and plenty of black sulphurets.

"There is a mill just finished and ready for work on the Stewart mine, the only mine prospected to any great depth.

'There is a superabundance of wood and water on all these claims for all mining and mechanical purposes.

"The maker of this report has lived in Sitka and worked on those mines for the last six years. The weather in the locality of those mines is very mild, no snow having fallen up to the time the writer left there, on the 15th of December last. Carrots, turnips, cabbages, etc., were at perfect maturity at that date, and not one frozen in the ground."

In a country as extended as Alaska, with its large rolling plains, wide valleys, and high mountains, there is necessarily a wide diversity of climate. In a general way it may be said that inland Alaska has an arctic winter and a tropical summer. At Fort Yukon the thermometer often goes above 100° in summer, and from 50° to 70° below zero in winter.

CLIMATE.

At Nulato on the Yukon River the fall of snow during the winter averages 8 feet, and frequently reaches 12 feet.

Along the immense southern coast and islands the climate is moist and warm.

The greatest cold recorded on the Island of Unalashka, by a Greek priest, during a period of five years, was zero of Fahrenheit ; extremest heat for the same time was 77°. The average for five years at 7 A.M. was 37°, 1 P.M., 40°, and 9 P.M., 36°. The average of weather for seven years was 53 all clear days, 1263 half clear, and 1235 all cloudy. It is very much the climate of north-western Scotland.

At St. Paul Harbor, Kadiak Island, the mean annual summer temperature is 54° and winter 29°. The coldest month, February, with the thermometer at 27°, and the warmest, July and August, with a mean temperature of 57°, the extremes being from 6° to 75°. The climate is that of southern Sweden and Norway. The annual rainfall is about 73 inches.

At Sitka, where, with the exception of a few short gaps, a record of the thermometer has been kept for 45 years, it has been found that the mean spring temperature has been 41° 2', summer 54° 6', autumn 44° 9', winter 32° 5', and for the entire year 43° 3' F. The greatest degree of heat recorded in these 45 years was 87° 8', and of cold 4° below zero. The thermometer has recorded below zero during only four of the 45 years, and above 80° during only seven of those years. The mean annual temperature for 45 years has ranged from 41° 3' to 46° 8', a difference of but 5° 5'. The annual rainfall 81 inches.

During a period of 43 years, there has been an average of 200 rainy or snowy days per year. The most favorable year was 1833, with 82 rainy and 32 snowy days, and the most unfavorable 1856, with 258 rainy and 27 snowy days.

During the winter of 1877 and 1878 the coldest night at Sitka only formed ice the thickness of a knife-blade on a barrel of rain-water under the eaves of a house.

At Fort Wrangell, owing to distance from the ocean and nearness to snow-covered mountains, the climate is colder than at Sitka. The mean temperatures are, for spring 40° 4′, for summer 57° 1′, autumn 43°, winter 28° 3′, and for the year 42° 2′. The annual rainfall about 65 inches. From these observations taken from the "Alaska Coast Pilot," Appendix 1, Meteorology, A.D. 1880, the surprising fact is brought to light that the winter climate of Southern Alaska for 45 years past has been the winter climate of the State of Kentucky and West Virginia.

This mild climate of Southern Alaska is due to the Japan Gulf Stream, the Kuro-Siwo, which first strikes the North American Continent at the Queen Charlotte Islands, in latitude 50° north. Here the stream divides, one portion going northward and westward along the coast of Alaska, and the other southward along the coast of British Columbia, Washington Territory, Oregon, and California, giving them their mild winter climate.

The former stream flowing northward has been named "the Alaska Current," and gives the great

HUNTING WALRUS.

southern coast of Alaska a winter climate as mild as that of one third of the United States.

Mr. Joseph Cook, in his celebrated Boston "Monday Lectures," thus refers to it :

"You will pardon me if I call attention to the reasons why Alaska is so warm. Everybody understands that the continents are tally-ho coaches driving toward the sunrise, and that the wind blows in the faces of those who sit on the front seats of coaches. The wind that bore Columbus across the Atlantic and Magellan across the Pacific blows in the faces of the tally-ho coaches of the continents, driving out of the sunset into the sunrise. As the trade winds in the tropics blow from east to west, at a speed often reaching fifteen or eighteen miles an hour, they produce a current in the ocean moving in the same direction across the tropical zone. When that current strikes the east side of a continent it divides, and part goes north and part goes south. As the portion moving toward the pole flows away

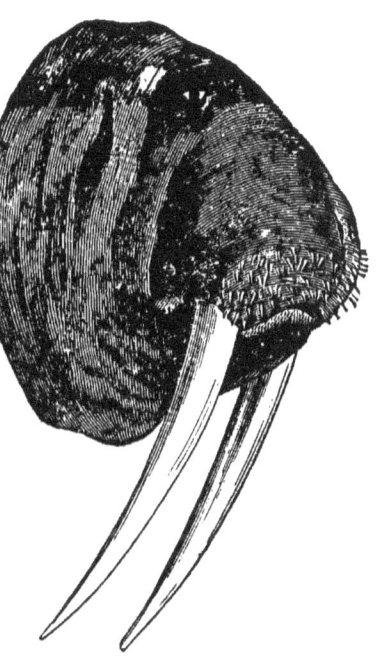

WALRUS HEAD.

from the tropics, it of course reaches a part of the earth moving with less rapidity than that from which it came. Everybody sees that the equator must revolve with far greater rapidity than the arctic circle, simply because it is larger and must turn around in the same time. The motion of the earth decreases from the equator to the pole. As the warm current passes from the equator to the North Sea in our Atlantic basin, it is constantly transferring itself to parallels that move less rapidly than those which it left at its last place of departure. The water does not at once lose the speed of eastern motion it had nearer the equator, and so slips eastward faster than the northern water it meets. Thus arises a translation of a great body of water toward the sunrise. In this way originates the gulf current, the cause of which was a mystery for ages. So in the Pacific Ocean, under the sweep of the trade winds and the influence of the difference of temperature between the torrid and the northern waters, there is produced an enormous equatorial current moving from east to west. On reaching the Asiatic coast and islands, a part of this vast stream goes north and a part south. The portion which goes north is of course always dropping into latitudes where the motion of the earth is less rapid, and therefore there is a translation of the waters toward America. Thus springs up a gulf current in the Pacific. (Guyot, 'Physical Geography,' p. 65.) It pours out of the East Indies as ours does out of the West Indies. It laves the coast of China and Japan, as ours does that of America. It is called the Japan Current, or Black

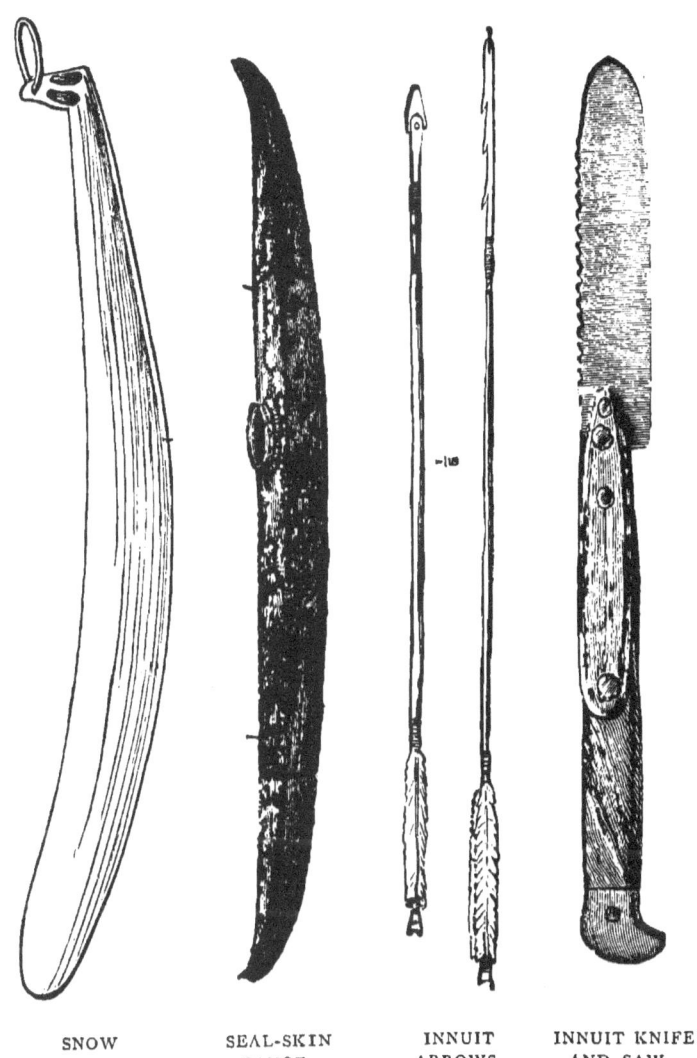

SNOW KNIFE.   SEAL-SKIN CANOE.   INNUIT ARROWS.   INNUIT KNIFE AND SAW.

water, and farther on has the name of the North Pacific Current. It divides at the westernmost end of the Aleutian Islands. A part of it runs through Bering Straits. That is the reason why the ice never drifts through those straits into the Pacific, and why the transit of steamers between China and the United States is likely to be free from icebergs. The larger part of the current goes south of the Aleutian archipelago and strikes our continent first on the coast of Alaska. As the Gulf Current warms England, so does the North Pacific Current warm Alaska and Oregon. But the Atlantic is more open to the Arctic Sea than the Pacific is, and so the latter current is less cooled by cold water from the north than the former."

With regard to Alaska, Mr. William H. Dall, of the Smithsonian Institution, writes after a trip to Europe : " I come back convinced, from personal inspection, that Alaska is a far better country than much of Great Britain and Norway, or even part of Prussia."

The routes of travel to Alaska are not very numerous. A steamer carrying the United States mail between Port Townsend, Washington Territory, and Fort Wrangell, and Sitka, Alaska, makes a monthly trip.

Two small steamers run at irregular intervals during the summer from Victoria, B. C., to Fort Wrangell, calling *en route* at the several trading-posts on the coast of British Columbia.

The country west of Sitka, including the Aleutian Islands and the great interior and main section of the

ROUTES OF TRAVEL. 61

Territory, is reached from San Francisco. So that a citizen of Oregon, in order to reach Kadiak, Unalashka, the Seal Islands, St. Michael, or the numerous villages on the Yukon River, is under the necessity of going by the way of San Francisco. From this latter place there is frequent communication with Western Alaska, and once a year with the central and northern sections.

ESKIMO HEAD.

CHAPTER II.

Population—Customs—Houses—Dances—Feasts—Cremation—
Religious Beliefs—Shamanism.

> " And they painted on the grave-posts
> Of the graves, yet unforgotten,
> Each his own ancestral *totem*,
> Each the symbol of his household—
> Figures of the bear and reindeer,
> Of the turtle, crane, or beaver."

MAJOR-GENERAL HALLECK, in his official report to the Secretary of War in 1869, gives the following statistics of the population of our lately-acquired Territory :

" Most writers make four general divisions of the natives of Alaska : 1st, the Koloshians ; 2d, the Kenaians ; 3d, the Aleuts ; 4th, the Eskimo. These are again subdivided into numerous tribes and families, which have been named sometimes from their places of residence or resort, and sometimes from other circumstances or incidents.

" 1. *The Koloshians.*—This name is given by the Russians to all the natives who inhabit the islands and coast from the latitude 54° 40' to the mouth of the Atna or Copper River. The Indians of the northern islands and northern coast of British Columbia be-

KEY LOW-TIK OR BASE DRUM DANCE.

HYDAS AND TONGAS PEOPLE. 65

long to the same stock, and their entire population was estimated by the early explorers at 25,000. The Koloshians in Alaska at the present time have been subdivided and classed as follows :

" The Hydas, who inhabit the southern part of Alexandria Archipelago. They have usually been hostile to the whites, and a few years ago captured a trading vessel and murdered the crew. They number about 600. These Indians are also called Kaigani

KEY-LOW-TIK AND KEN-TOON.

and Kliavakans ; the former being near Kaigan Harbor, and the latter near the Gulf of Kliavakan.

"In the same archipelago are the Hennegas, who live near Cape Pole, and the Chatsinas, who occupy the northern portion of the principal island. They are said to be peaceful, and to number about 500 each, in all about 1000.

"The Tongas, who live on Tongas Island and on the north side of Dixon Inlet. A branch of this tribe, called the Foxes, now under a separate chief, live near Cape Fox. The two branches together number about 500.

"The Stickeens, who live on the Stickeen River and the islands near its mouth. Although represented as at the present time peaceable, a few years ago they captured a trading vessel and murdered the crew. They number about 1000.

"The Kakus, or Kakes, who live on Kupreanoff Island, having their principal settlement near the north-western side. These Indians have long been hostile to the whites, making distant warlike incursions in their canoes. They have several times visited Puget Sound, and in 1857 murdered the collector of customs at Port Townsend. They number altogether about 1200.

"The Kuius, who have several villages on the bays and inlets of Kuiu Island, between Cape Division and Prince Frederick's Sound. They number in all about 800.

"The Kootznoos or Kooshnoos, who live near Kootznoo Head, at the mouth of Hood's Bay, Admiralty Island. They number about 800.

"The Awks, who live along Douglas' Channel and near the mouth of the Tahko River. They have a bad reputation, and number about 800.

"The Sundowns and Tahkos, who live on the main land from Port Houghton to the Tahko River. They number about 500.

"The Chilcatds or Chilkahts, living on Lynn Channel and the Chilkaht River. They are warlike, and have heretofore been hostile to all whites, but at

ESKIMO SNOW-HOUSE, ALASKA.

SITKA AND KENAIAN PEOPLE.

present manifest a disposition to be friendly. They muster about 2000.

"The Hoodsuna-hoos, who live near the head of Chatham Straits. There are also small settlements of them near Port Frederick, and at some other points. They number about 1000.

"The Hunnas or Hooniaks, who are scattered along the main land from Lynn Canal to Cape Spencer. Their number is about 1000.

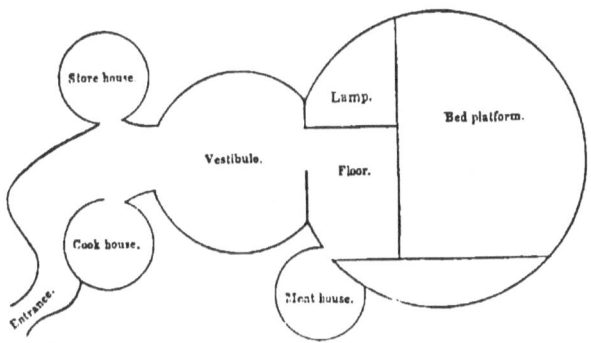

DIAGRAM OF ESKIMO SNOW-HOUSE.

"The Sitkas, or Indians on Baranoff Island, who were at first opposed to the change of flags, but have since become friendly. These are estimated by General Davis at about 1200.

"If we add to these the scattering families and tribes on the islands not above enumerated, and the Kyacks, who live south of Copper River, we shall have from 12,000 to 15,000 as the whole number of Koloshians in the Territory.

"2. *The Kenaians.*—This name, derived from the peninsula of Kenai, which lies between Cook's Inlet and Prince William's Sound, has been applied to all the Indians who occupy the country north of Copper River and west of the Rocky Mountains, except the Aleutes and Esquimaux. The employés of the telegraph company represent them as peaceful and well disposed. They, however, are ready to avenge any affront or wrong. I have not sufficient data to give the names, locations, or numbers of the several tribes of these people. Their whole number is usually estimated at 25,000.

"3. *The Aleuts.*—This term more properly belongs to the natives of the Aleutian Islands, but it has been applied also to those of the Shumagin and Kadiak groups, and to the southern Eskimo, whom they greatly resemble. They are generally kind and well disposed, and not entirely wanting

ESKIMO HUNTER, ALASKA.

in industry. By the introduction of schools and churches among these people the Russians have done much toward reducing them to a state of civilization. As might be expected from the indefinite character of the lines separating them from the Eskimos, the estimates of their numbers are conflicting, varying from 4000 to 10,000. Probably the lowest number would comprise all the inhabitants of the Aleutian Islands Proper, while if we include the other groups and the Peninsula of Alaska, and the country bordering on Bristol Bay, the whole number may reach as high as 10,000.

" 4. *The Eskimos.*—These people, who constitute the remainder of the population of Alaska, inhabit the coasts of Bering's Sea and of the Arctic Ocean, and the interior country north, and including the northern branches of the Yukon River. The Kenaians are said to hold the country along the more southerly branches of that river. The character of the Alaskian Eskimo does not essentially differ from that of the same race

ESKIMO WOMAN, ALASKA.

in other parts of the world. They are low in the scale of humanity, and number about 20,000. These estimates make the entire Indian population of Alaska about 60,000."

William H. Dall, in "North American Ethnology," Vol. i., gives the following enumeration :

TINNEH.
(WESTERN.)

Kaiyŭhkhotănă	2,000
Koyŭkŭkhotănă	500
Unăkotănă	300

(KŬTCHIN.)

Tenan-kŭtchin	400
Tennŭth-kŭtchin, extinct.	
Tătsăh-kŭtchin, extinct.	
Kŭtchă kŭtchin	250
Nătsit-kŭtchin	150
Vŭnta-kŭtchin.	
Tŭkkŭth-kŭtchin.	
Hăn kŭtchin.	
Tŭtchone-kŭtchin.	
Tehănin-kŭtchin	1,000

(EASTERN.)

Abbăto-tenă.	
Mauvais Monde (Nehaunees).	
Acheto-tinneh.	
Dăho-tenă.	
Tăhko-tinneh.	
" Chilkaht-tena."	
Ah-tena	1,500

BONE COMB.

T'LINKETS.
(YAKŬTATS.)

"Yakŭtats"	250

(KWAN.)

Chilkăht-kwăn	1,300
Sitkă-kwăn	2,200
Stăkhin-kwăn	1,500

COLYER'S ESTIMATE OF THE PEOPLE. 73

(KYGAHNI.)
Kygāhni.. 300

(NASSES.)
Nasse Indians.
Chimsyūns.

Alaska Indians.................................. 11,650
Alaska Orarians (Coast Indians)................ 14,054

Total native population........................ 25,704
Add Russians................................... 50
" Half-breeds or Creoles...................... 1,500
" Citizens.................................... 150

27,404

The reader will notice the wide discrepancy between the foregoing estimates. No census of the country has ever been taken, and so large a portion is still unexplored that it would be practically impossible to secure a census. The Russian officials claimed at the time of the transfer a population of about 66,000.

The Hon. Vincent Colyer, Special Indian Commissioner to Alaska, in closing his report, says: "I do not hesitate to say that if three fourths of them (Alaska Indians) were landed in New York as coming from Europe, they would be selected as among the most intelligent of the many worthy emigrants who daily arrive at that port."

Ivan Petroff, Esq., editor and proprietor of the *Alaska Appeal*, gives the following enumeration of the Aleutian Islands for 1879:

Unalashka, 304 Russians, Creoles, and Aleuts, and 5 white men, in four villages; Akutan, 140 Aleuts and Creoles; Atka, 207 Aleuts and Creoles, 1 white man ; Umnak, 117 Aleuts and Creoles. From Atka to Attu, 600 miles, 10 to 15 islands, with 170 Aleuts. Shumagin Islands—Unga, 160 Aleuts, 69 Creoles, and 13 white men ; Belkovsky, 193 Creoles, 80 Aleuts, and 2 white men ; Nikolaievsk, 31 Aleuts ; Protasof, 53 Creoles and 67 Aleuts ; Cook's Inlet, 620 Creoles and 4 white men.

The principal villages are :

Unalashka.—This is the refitting station for all vessels passing between the Pacific Ocean and Bering's Sea. It is also the most important trading post of the Alaska Commercial Company. "The village straggles along a narrow sand-spit formed by the water of the bay and a shallow creek, and begins with the substantial wharf, warehouses, and dwelling-houses of the Commercial Company. The centre of the town is occupied by the Russian church and the residence of the Greek priest, the neatest, best furnished and most comfortable house in the Territory, and the eastern end is composed chiefly of the half-subterranean 'barabaras' of the Aleuts and the new houses of the rival trading firm. The best hunters have been furnished by the company with comfortable cottages, which they occupy rent free."

St. Paul's Harbor, on Kadiak Island.—This was at one time the capital of Russian America and the chief seat of operations. The island was discovered in 1763 by Gotloff. In 1783 it was occupied by Shelikoff, who erected the first trading post. The settlement at St. Paul's Harbor was made in 1792. In 1794 eleven monks arrived to establish missions, and in 1796 the first Russo-Greek church was

HUNTING MUSK-OX.

erected. Joasaph, Elder of the Augustin Friars, was made bishop. In 1799 it was made head-quarters of the Russian-American Fur Company and capital of Alaska. Schools and a hospital were also established. Its prosperity waned with the transfer of the capital to Sitka.

Sitka.—This village is described in chapter 7.

Fort Wrangell.—This village of one hundred houses is on the northwestern coast of Wrangell Island, near the mouth of the Stickeen river. Owing to the extensive gold mines at Cassair, on the Stickeen river, it has become the chief business centre of Alaska. The trade of the mines Wrangell is at the end of ocean and commencement of river navigation. An ocean steamer runs between Portland and Wrangell and two between Victoria and Wrangell, and two small river steamers run on the Stickeen river between Wrangell and the Mines. The coast of Wrangell and the mouth of Stickeen river was first visited by the American ship Atahualpa of Boston, in 1802, three years before Lewis and Clark descended the Columbia. The permanent population is about one hundred whites and Russians, and five hundred Indians. Besides these there is a large winter population of miners, and a floating Indian population of from 500 to 700 more, there sometimes being from

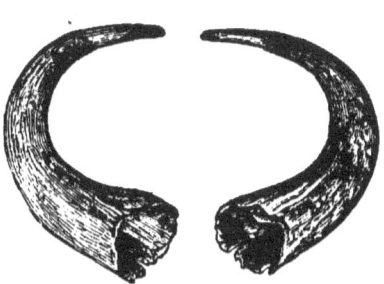

HORNS OF MUSK-OX.

2000 to 3000 Indians in the place. It is on the great highway of the Indians to and from the mines, also to their hunting and fishing.

Along the main coast and upon the islands of the Alexander Archipelago are seven or eight tribes speaking a common language called the Thlinket. These tribes dwell mainly in sixteen villages.

Like other Alaska tribes, they have several chiefs, one of whom is head chief. Upon all public occasions they are seated according to their rank. This rank is distinguished by the height of a pole erected in front of their houses. The greater the chief the higher his pole. Some of these poles are over 100 feet high. Mr. Duncan, the missionary, relates that upon one occasion a chief of the Naass River Indians put up a pole higher than his rank would allow. The friends of the head chief made fight with guns, and the over-ambitious one was shot in the arm, which led him quickly to shorten his pole.

The Indians are again subdivided into various families, each of which have their family badge. These badges, or *totems* among the Thlinkets are the raven (yehl), the wolf (kahanukh), the whale (koostan-ine), and the eagle (chethl'). Their emblems are marked on the houses, canoes, household utensils, ornaments, and even clothing of the people. These crests or badges extend through different tribes, and their members have a closer relation to one another than the tribal connection. For instance, members of the same tribe may marry, but not members of the same badge. Thus a wolf may not marry into the wolf family, but may into that of the whale,

TOTEM POLES, FORT WRANGELL.

In front of their leading houses and at their burial-places are sometimes immense timbers covered with carvings. Those who attended the Centennial Exhibition will remember such posts. These are the genealogical records of the family. The child usually takes the *totem* of the mother. For instance, at the bottom of a post may be the carving of a whale, over that a raven, a wolf, and an eagle—

STATUE OF THE CHIEF'S SON.   CARVED BEAR.   FORT WRANGELL.

signifying that the great-grandfather of the present occupant of the house on his mother's side belonged to the whale family, the grandfather to the raven family, the father to the wolf family, and he himself to the eagle family. These standards are from two to five feet in diameter, and often over 60 feet in height, and sometimes cost from $1000 to $2000, including the gifts and entertainments that attend their dedication. Formerly the entrance to the house was a hole through this standard, but latterly they are commencing to have regular doors hung on hinges. Among the Stickeens these badge trees or *totems* are usually removed to one side of the door.

Their houses are generally built along the beach at the edge of high tide. They are from 25 to 40 feet square, without a window, the only openings being a small door for entrance and a hole in the roof for the escape of the smoke. The door is three or four feet above the ground level, and opens inside upon a broad platform, which extends around the four sides. This platform contains their rolls of blankets, bedding, and other stores. Some of the houses have a second platform inside the first, and a few steps lower. Then a few more steps down is the inside square on the ground floor, which is also planked, with the exception of about four feet square in the centre, where the fire is built on the ground. Some few have a small inside room, looking as if it were a portion of the cabin of a vessel. The walls, and frequently roofs, are made of cedar plank, from two to five feet wide, and two to three inches thick. These planks are made by first splitting the trees into great planks, then smoothing them down with a small adze.

The people have to a great extent adopted an American style of dress, the universal ready-made clothing store having already found its way to that coast.

The beach is lined with their large canoes. These are from twenty to thirty feet long, and made out of one solid log of cedar or cypress. Some of the largest are from sixty to seventy-five feet long and eight to ten feet wide, and will carry one hundred people.

One was on exhibition at the Centennial Exhibition. The operation of making them is thus described : " Having selected a sound tree and cut it the desired length, the outside is first shaped, then the tree is hollowed out till the shell is of proper thickness ; this is done with a tool resembling a grubbing-hoe or narrow adze with a short handle. It is then filled with water, which is heated by throwing in hot stones. The canoe is then covered with a canvas to keep the steam in ; this softens the timber, and the sides are distended by cross sticks to the desired breadth at the centre, and tapering toward the ends in lines of beautiful symmetry. It is finished off with a highly ornamental figure-head, and the bulwarks strengthened by a fancy covering board."

Their food consists largely of berries and fish. Large quantities of salmon are smoked and put away for future use. They also prepare large quantities of fish-oil.

Some years ago a party of them, having seen the cooks on ship mix flour and bake it into bread, got possession of a barrel of lime from a shipwrecked vessel. A portion of this was mixed as they had seen the cook do it, and baked and boiled and boiled and baked, but to their great disgust nothing eatable came from it.

Many of them paint their faces with lampblack and oil, which gives them a very repulsive appearance.

84 MANUFACTURES.

They have a great variety of household utensils made from the horns of mountain sheep and goats, from ivory, and from wood. These are elaborately carved with their *totemic* or heraldic signs. Indeed, they excel in carving. They also excel in the manufacture of baskets, mats, dishes, hats, etc., out of the inner bark of the cedar. These baskets will hold

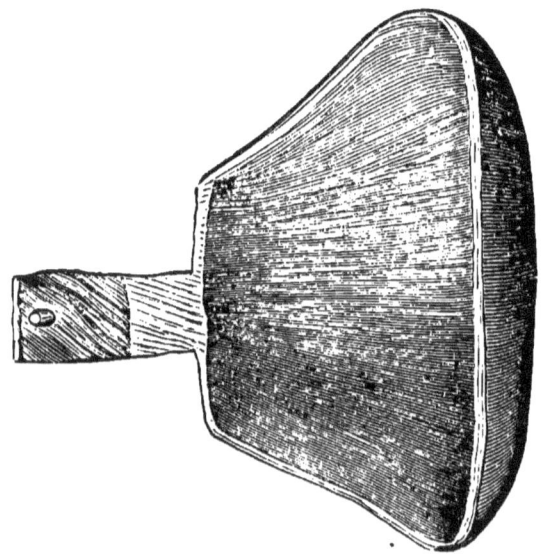

LADLE FROM HORN OF MUSK-OX.

water, and in the olden times, before the introduction of iron kettles, they were used for boiling. This was done, not by placing the basket of water into or over the fire, but by heating stones and placing them in the basket.

Mr. W. H. Dall, in his "Alaska and its Resources," gives the following customs of the people:

MARRIAGE. 85

"Polygamy is common among the rich. Upon arriving at a marriageable age the lower lip of the girl is pierced and a silver pin inserted, the flat head of the pin being in the mouth, and the pin projecting through the lip over the chin. Many of them, men as well as women, wear a silver ring in the nose as well as the ears.

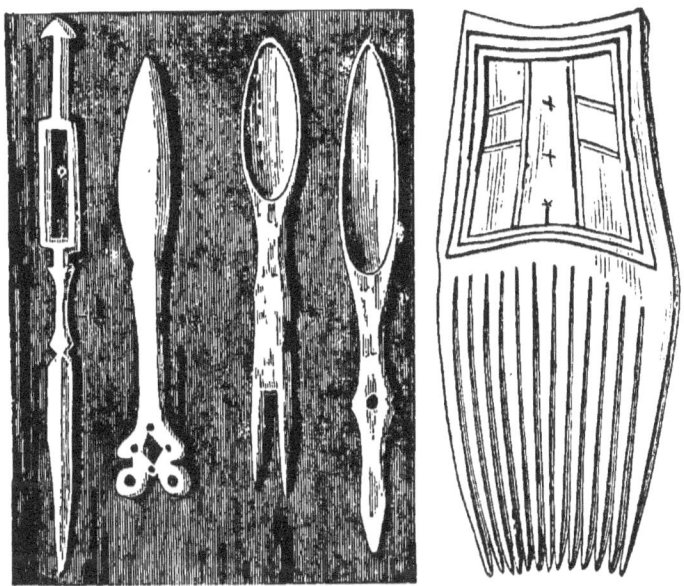

IVORY KNIVES, FORKS, AND COMB.

"A man wanting a wife sends a message to that effect to the girl's relations. If he receives a favorable answer he sends them all the presents he can procure. Upon the appointed day he goes to her father's house and sits down on the door-step with his back to the house.

"The relations who have assembled then sing a marriage song, at the close of which furs and calico are laid across the floor, and the girl is escorted over them from the corner where she has been sitting, and takes her seat by the side of the man.

"The dancing, singing, and eating are kept up by the guests, until they are tired. In these festivities the couple take no part. They then fast for two days, and after a slight repast fast two days more.

DEER-SKIN BOOTS.

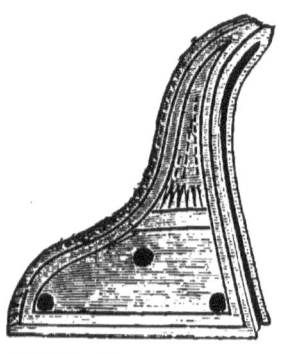

CARVED ORNAMENT TO A CANOE-HEAD.

Four weeks afterward they come together and are recognized as husband and wife. Perhaps if there was more fasting upon similar occasions among Americans there would be fewer divorces. After marriage the silver pin is removed from the woman's lip, and a spool-shaped plug, called a labret, about three quarters of an inch long, is substituted in its place. As she grows older, larger ones are inserted, so that an old woman may have one two inches in diameter. When a husband dies, his brother or sister's son must marry the widow. A refusal to do this has led to wars. If there are no male relations of the husband, the widow can choose for herself.

"They consider corporeal punishment as a great disgrace, and only chastise the child who refuses to take its daily bath.

"Theft is not considered as a crime, but the loser may demand restitution if the thief is discovered.

"Murder demands blood for blood; if not that of the actual murderer, at least one of the tribe or family to which he belongs.

"Family feuds are not uncommon, and sometimes result in duels. The duellists are dressed in armor of raw moose or bear hide, or thin strips of wood laced together. They wear heavy wooden helmets painted or carved with their *totemic* emblems. The combat is carried on with knives, and accompanied with songs by the bystanders. At a conclusion of peace, either between two tribes or two members of a family, hostages are exchanged. These are obliged to eat with their left hands for a certain period, as they had carried weapons in the right hand during the combat. Each hostage has two companions of equal rank assigned to him by the tribe which holds him.

"Their method of war is an ambush or surprise. The prisoners are made slaves, and the dead are scalped. The scalps are woven into a kind of garter by the victor. During war they use red paint on their faces, and powder their hair with red earth and the down of birds.

"The talent for carving in wood and bone possessed by the Thlinkets has long been a matter of remark. Before the introduction of iron by the Russians they were unacquainted with it, but used tools of stone or native copper. At present many of them have some knowledge of working in iron. They purchase large files of the traders, of which they make peculiar bayonet-shaped knives. Those of native copper were of similar form, and both are frequently ornamented

TOMB OF THE CHIEF'S SON.   THREE COLOSSAL FROGS CARVED IN WOOD, FT. WRANGELL.

with *totemic* emblems. They are fond of silver and other white metals, which they prefer to brass or gold. They wear ear-rings and other ornaments of their own manufacture from silver half-dollars.

"Bows and arrows seem to have disappeared, as they have been well supplied for years by the traders with iron spears or pikes and flint-lock guns.

"Their festivals consist of dancing, singing, and feasting. The dances and songs are all emblematic,

FUNERAL CEREMONIES.

and the Thlinket prides himself above all on his proficiency in these accomplishments. The songs are remarkable for their rhythm."

In their villages, scattered between the houses and the higher land back of them, are a number of boxes about five feet by two in size, raised on four posts a few feet from the ground. Also small frame houses like an old-fashioned smokehouse four feet square.

INNUIT GRAVE.

These are the graves of the chiefs and shamans (sorcerers). One of them at Fort Wrangell was surmounted by a wooden figure of a whale ten feet long; another had a figure of an immense bear. Others had the genealogy of the dead painted upon them.

"The bodies of the dead are disjointed and burned. The funeral ceremonies of the wealthy often last four days. Dead slaves are cast into the sea. They believe in the transmigration of souls from one body

INGALIK GRAVE.

to another, but not to animals. And the wish is often expressed that in the next change they may be born into this or that powerful family. Those whose bodies are burned are supposed to be warm in the next world, and the others cold. If slaves are sacrificed at their burial, it relieves their owners from work in the next world.

"Poor people take their dead in a boat to some distant spot and burn them there. Some time after the death of a Thlinket the members of the family who belong to other *totems* are invited to a feast. The body is put on a funeral pile before the relations and burned. The guests accompany the ceremony with dismal cries. They sometimes burn their hair in the fire, or cut it off and smear themselves with ashes. Among the Hydahs they cut themselves with knives and stones. The guests who are of the same *totem* as the wife then enter the house, while the near relatives come in, disfigured and leaning on long staves, and weep or sing in the middle of the floor. These ceremonies last four days, with short intervals for eating. Several slaves were formerly killed, the number varying with the wealth of the dead man. After four days the relations wash and paint their faces. Presents are made to the guests who have assisted, and food is distributed, which concludes the ceremony."

EKOGMUT GRAVE.

"The next heir is the younger brother or sister's son. The ashes of the dead are placed in curiously painted boxes near the house."

One beautiful morning in 1879, Dr. Kendall and myself went up the beach at Fort Wrangell to see a vegetable garden recently opened by Mr. Davidson. At its upper end we saw a white sheet stretched between two poles and looking as if it might be intended for a scare crow. Upon inquiry we found that it contained the ashes of a boy who was drowned the week before. His friends had promised Rev. Mr. Young that he should have a Christian burial. But during Saturday night they took the body up the beach, and early Sabbath morning burned it.

Several large dry sticks were laid side by side upon the beach. Upon these was placed the body of the boy. Other sticks were piled over the body and the whole set on fire amid the wails and superstitious incantations of hired mourners.

In about an hour the body was consumed. After the fire had cooled down, the ashes were carefully gathered up and placed in a basket until a suitable box could be carved for their permanent preservation. When all was ready, an old Indian woman, bowed down with age and infirmities, took up the basket and started for a pine-tree, which had previously been selected for the purpose. She was followed by the mourners and friends with bowed heads and loud wails of sorrow. At the base of the tree two poles, about eight feet high, were driven into the ground two feet apart. The basket containing the ashes was tied between these poles, and a muslin bag, like a large pillow-slip, pulled down over the poles and basket and sewed up at the bottom. On the outside of the sheet is sometimes rudely painted a face, through which the spirit of the departed is supposed to look out upon the bay.

Morning and evening the parents of the boy come out from their hut, and turning their faces to the north utter loud cries of distress. This will be kept up several months.

A writer in vol. iii., "North American Ethnology," says:

"I witnessed a scene of cremation on Bear River that was one of the most hideous and awful spectacles of which the human mind can conceive. The mourners leaped and howled around the burning pyre like demons, holding long poles in their hands, which, ever and anon they thrust into the seething, blistering corpse, with dismal cries of '*Wu-wu-wu!*' On American River, after the body is reduced to a little smouldering lump, the women draw it out of the fire, then each one in succession takes it in her hands, holds it high above her head, and walks around the pyre, uttering doleful wails and ululations. They also have a dance for the dead (*tsi'-pi ka-mi'-ni*, ' the weeping dance '). It always occurs about the last of August, beginning in the evening and lasting until daybreak. They bring together a great quantity of food, clothing, baskets, and whatever other things they believe the dead require in the other world. Everything is bought or made new for the occasion; the food is fresh and good, the clothing is newly

CREMATION.

MOURNING FOR THE DEAD. 95

woven and fine, the ornaments are the best they can procure. These are hung on a semicircle of boughs or small trees, cut and set in the ground leafless, the smaller and lighter articles at the top, twelve or fifteen feet high, and the larger toward the bottom or lying on the ground. In the centre burns a great fire, and hard by are the graves. On the opposite side of the fire from the offerings there is a screen made of bushes, with blankets hung over them to reflect the light of the fire brilliantly on the offerings, which glitter like a row of Christmas-trees. They seat themselves on the graves, men and squaws together, as the twilight closes in around them, and begin a mournful wailing, crying, and ululation for the dead of the year. After a time they rise and form a circle round the fire, between it and the offerings, and commence a dance, accompanied by that hoarse, deathly rattle of the Indian chant which sounds so eldritch and so terrible to the civilized ear. Heavily the dancing and the singing go on from hour to hour, and now and then a few pounds of provisions, a string of shell-money, or some article is taken down from the espaliers and cast into the flames. All through the night the funereal dance goes on without cessation; wilder and more frantic grows the chanting, swifter becomes the motion of the dancers, and faster and faster the offerings are hurled upon the blazing heap. The savage transports wax amain. With frenzied yells and whoops they leap in the flickering firelight like demons—a terrible spectacle. Now some squaw, if not restrained, would fling herself headlong into the burning mass. Another will lie down and calmly sleep amid the extraordinary commotion for two hours, then arise and join as wildly as before in the frightful orgies. But still the espaliers are not emptied, and as the morning stars grow dim and daybreak is close at hand, with one frantic rush, yelling, they seize down the residue of the clothing (the clothing is mostly reserved until near morning) and whirl it into the flames, lest the first gray streak of dawn should appear before the year-long hunger of the ghosts is appeased."

At the funeral of chiefs the traditions and history of the tribe are rehearsed. If these ceremonies are not conducted properly, the water of death swallows up the departed soul, or it is lost in the forests. But if conducted properly, the chief of the gods speaks the word, and the "water of death is small," and the soul is carried to a place of rest or forgetfulness. Then after a long time it comes back to some descendant on its sister's side, and lives another life. To such superstitions these people are bound body and soul.

Dall thus writes concerning the religious beliefs of the Thlinkets:

"Their religion is a feeble polytheism. Yehl is the maker of wood and waters. He put the sun, moon, and stars in their places. He lives in the east, near the head-waters of the Naass River. He makes himself known in the east wind 'Ssankheth,' and his abode is 'Nassshak-yehl.'

"There was a time when men groped in the dark in search of the world. At that time a Thlinket lived

EVIL SPIRITS.

who had a wife and sister. He loved the former so much that he did not permit her to work. Eight little red birds, called kun, were always around her. One day she spoke to a stranger. The little birds flew and told the jealous husband, who prepared to make a box to shut his wife up. He killed all his sister's children because they looked at his wife. Weeping, the mother went to the sea-shore. A whale saw her and asked the cause of her grief, and when informed, told her to swallow a small stone from the beach and drink some sea-water. In eight months she had a son, whom she hid from her brother. This son was Yehl.

"At that time the sun, moon, and stars were kept by a rich chief in separate boxes, which he allowed no one to touch. Yehl, by strategy, secured and opened these boxes, so that the moon and stars shone in the sky. When the sun box was opened, the people, astonished at the unwonted glare, ran off into the mountains, woods, and even into the water, becoming animals or fish. He also provided fire and water. Having arranged everything for the comfort of the Thlinkets, he disappeared where neither man nor spirit can penetrate.

"There are an immense number of minor spirits called yekh. Each shaman has his own familiar spirits that do his bidding, and others on whom he may call in certain emergencies. These spirits are divided into three classes—Khiyekh (the upper ones), Takhi-yekh (land spirits), and Tekhi-yekh (sea spirits) The first are the spirits of the brave killed in war, and dwelling in the north. Hence a great display of northern lights is looked upon as an omen of war. The second and third are the spirits of those who died in the common way, and who dwell in Takhan-khov. The ease with which these latter reach their appointed place is dependent on the conduct of their relations in mourning for them. In addition to these spirits every one has his yekh, who is always with him, except in cases when the man becomes exceedingly bad, when the yekh leaves him.

"These spirits only permit themselves to be conjured by the sound of a drum or rattle. The last is usually made in the shape of a bird, hollow, and filled with small stones. These are used at all festivities and whenever the spirits are wanted."

As the good spirits, from the very nature of the case, will not harm them, the Indians pay but little attention to them. They give their chief attention to propitiating the evil spirits, so that their religion practically resolves itself into devil-worship or demonolatry. This is called Shamanism, or the giving of offerings to evil spirits to prevent them from doing mischief to the offerer. It is said to have been the old religion of the Tartar race before the introduction of Buddhism, and is still that of the Siberians. Indeed, long ago Paul declared: " the things which the Gentiles sacrifice, they sacrifice to *devils*, and not to God " (I Cor. 10:20). The one whose office it is to perform these rites is called a shaman, and is the sorcerer or medicine-man of the tribes. The shaman has control, not only of the spirits, but, through the spirits, of diseases, of the elements, and of nature, he holds in his power success or misfortune, bless-

ing or cursing. "The honor and respect," says
Dall, "with which a shaman is regarded depend on
the number of spirits under his control, who, properly employed, contribute largely to his wealth. For

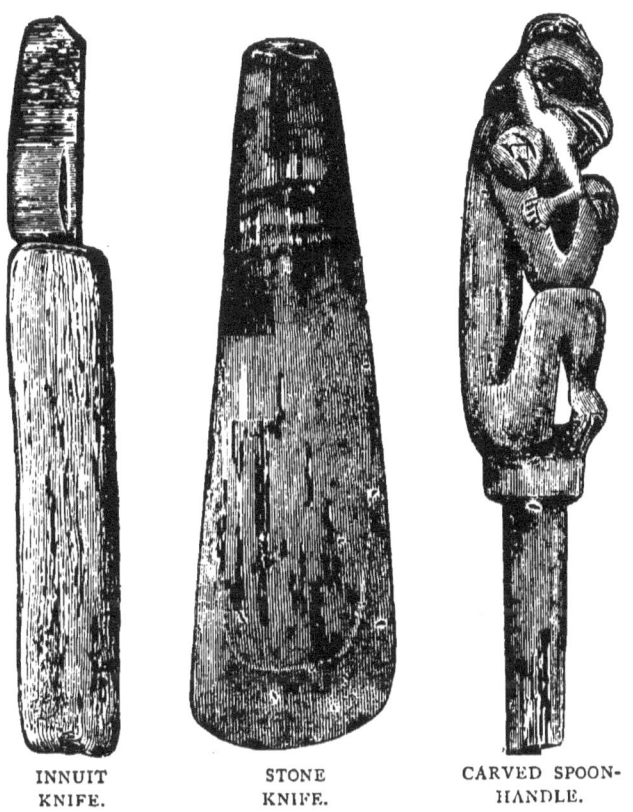

| INNUIT KNIFE. | STONE KNIFE. | CARVED SPOON-HANDLE. |

every one of them he has a name and certain songs.
Sometimes the spirits of his ancestors come to his
assistance and increase his power, so that it is believed he can throw his spirits into other people who

do not believe in his art. Those unfortunate wretches to whom this happens suffer from horrible fits and paroxysms.

"When the shaman is sick his relations fast to promote his recovery. His command is law. The shamans long since forbade the eating of whale's flesh and blubber, one of the greatest delicacies among the neighboring tribes ; and to this day it is regarded with abhorrence by the Thlinkets.

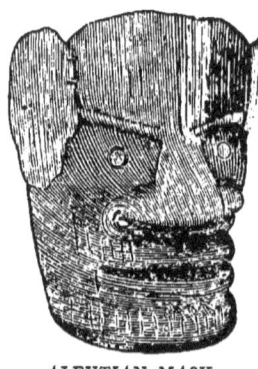

ALEUTIAN MASK.

"The shaman has a large amount of paraphernalia. This includes wooden masks, one for each spirit, carved and carefully painted. These are distinct from the masks used by all the Thlinkets in their dances and festivals.

"The hair of the shaman must never be cut. After his death, as was mentioned previously, his body is not burned, but deposited in a wooden box on four high posts. For the first night it remains lying in the corner where he died ; but on the following day it is removed to the opposite corner, and this is continued until the body has visited each of the four corners of the house. All the inmates of the house fast meanwhile.

"On the fifth day the body, dressed in the garb of his profession, is bound to a board. Two ivory or bone wands, which the shaman used in his performances, are placed, the one in the cartilage of the nose and the other in the hair, which is tied together.

SHAMANISM.

"The head is covered with a piece of basket-work, and the body is carried to its final resting-place, always on the shore. Every time a Thlinket paddles by the remains he throws an offering, as a little tobacco, in the water, that he may by this means find favor in the eyes of the dead man.

"One example of the manner in which shamanism is practised will suffice.

"On the day appointed for the exhibition of his

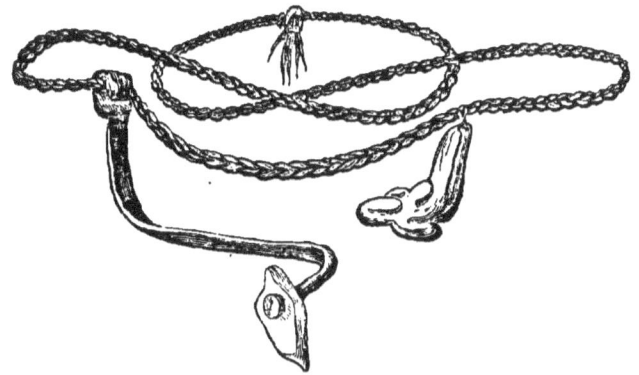

INNUIT BONE CHARM.

power, his relations, who act the part of a chorus of singers, are obliged to fast. Nay, more than that: they are obliged to use a feather as an emetic, and free themselves entirely from such gross material substances as food.

"The performance commences at sunset and lasts till sunrise. All who wish to participate assemble in the lodge or hut of the shaman, where they join in a song, to which time is beaten on a drum. Dressed in his paraphernalia, with a mask over his face, the shaman rushes round and round the fire, which is burning in the centre of the lodge; he keeps his eyes directed toward the opening in the roof, and keeps time to the drum with violent motions of his limbs and body. These movements gradually become more convulsive; his eyes roll till the whites alone are visible. Suddenly he stops, looks intently at the drum, and utters loud cries. The singing ceases, and all eyes are directed toward him, and all ears strained to catch the utterances which are supposed to be inspired. These ceremonies comprise the whole art of shamanism among the Thlinkets. The spirits of the different classes appear to the shaman in different forms. By changing the masks he places himself 'en rapport' with the spirit to which each mask is dedicated. It is believed that this spirit inspires for the moment all the utterances of the shaman, who is for the moment unconscious."

Bancroft, in his "Native Races on the Pacific Coast," thus speaks of shamanism: "Thick, black clouds, portentous of evil, hang threateningly over the savage during his entire life. Genii murmur in the flowing river; in the rustling branches of trees are heard the breathings of the gods; goblins dance in the vapory twilight, and demons howl in the darkness. All these beings are hostile to man, and must be propitiated by gifts and prayers and sacrifices; and the religious worship of some of the tribes includes practices which are frightful in their atrocity. Here, for example, is a rite of sorcery as practised among the Haidahs, one of the northern nations:

"When the salmon season is over, and the provisions of winter have been stored away, feasting and conjuring begin. The chief—who seems to be principal sorcerer, and indeed to possess little authority save for his connection with the preterhuman powers—goes off to the loneliest and wildest retreat he knows of or can discover in the mountains or forests, and half starves himself there for some weeks, till he is worked up to a frenzy of religious insanity, and the *nawloks*—fearful beings of some kind not human—consent to communicate with him by voices or otherwise. During all this observance the chief is called *taamish*, and woe to the unlucky Haidah who happens by chance so much as to look on him during its continuance! Even if the *taamish* do not instantly slay the intruder, his neighbors are certain to do so when the thing comes to their knowledge, and if the victim attempt to conceal the affair, or do not himself confess it, the most cruel tortures are added to his fate. At last the inspired demoniac returns to his village, naked save a bear-skin or a ragged blanket, with a chaplet on his head and a red band of alder-bark about his neck. He springs on the first person he meets, bites out and swallows one or more mouthfuls of the man's living flesh wherever he can fix his teeth, then rushes to another and another, repeating his revolting meal till he falls into a torpor from his sudden and half-masticated surfeit of flesh. For some days after this he lies in a kind of coma, ' like an overgorged beast of prey,' as Dunn says ; the same observer adding that his breath during that time is ' like an exhalation from the grave.' The victims of this ferocity dare not resist the bite of the *taamish*; on the contrary, they are sometimes willing to offer themselves to the ordeal, and are always proud of its scars."

All the Alaska Indians are held in abject fear by the conjurers or medicine-men.

During the visit of the Rev. Dr. Henry Kendall and party to Alaska, in 1879, the Christian Indians at Fort Wrangell, in order to testify their joy at our visit, and also to show us what were their customs before the missionary came, gave a series of entertainments.

One afternoon we were invited to the house of Toy-a-att, a leading chief and Christian, to witness a representation of some of their national customs.

When everything was prepared, dressed in a hunting-shirt, with face blackened and spear in hand, Toy-a-att appeared in the war-dance. Retiring with much applause he reappeared in the form of a wolf, and, with mask, rolling eyes and snapping teeth, gave the dance of the "invocation of the spirits for success in hunting." Then he put on a horrible mask to represent the devil, and with hideous rattles gave the devil or Tamanamus dance. Then with dress and mask, and large hat with tinkling bells on the rim and eider-down in the crown (which down he showered around the room as blessings upon his guests), and rattles in his hands, he gave us the religious dance of the shamans or medicine-men.

After a series of national dances he came out and made a speech, apologizing for the feebleness of his representations. In his red cloth shirt, covered with mythological emblems worked in white pearl buttons and beads, his embroidered and painted deer-skin blanket thrown over one shoulder and gathered under the other arm, with one foot advanced and erect head, with graceful and expressive gestures, he spoke in substance as follows:

"When I was a young man I danced vigorously; now, since I have become a Christian, I have almost forgotten how. When I was young I was a great fighter; now I have learned from Christianity to fight no more. Christianity has changed us. Formerly we thought the crow made us, and made these mountains, and the water, and everything; now we know God made it. They lie who say no God made the sun, moon, light, darkness. God made them all with his strong arm. Our fathers were foolish, and said the crow

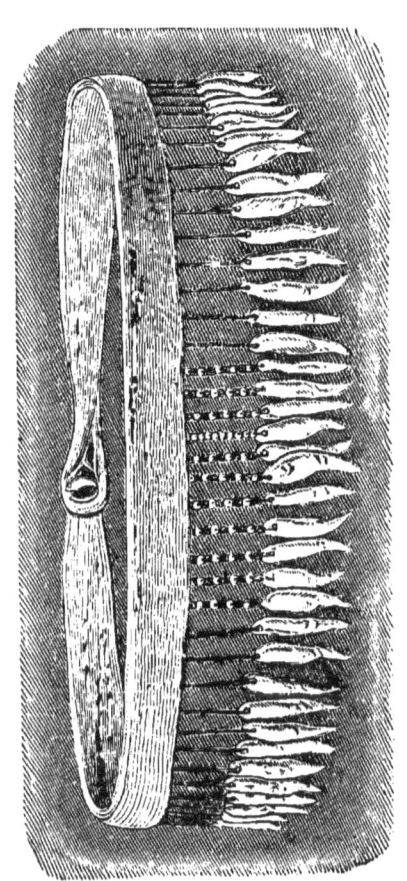

SEAL-TOOTH HEAD-DRESS.

made it; now we know better; we know that God made them.

"My brothers, I thank you. You come into this house to see how we used to do. You laugh at what we used to do. We were foolish. Now we know

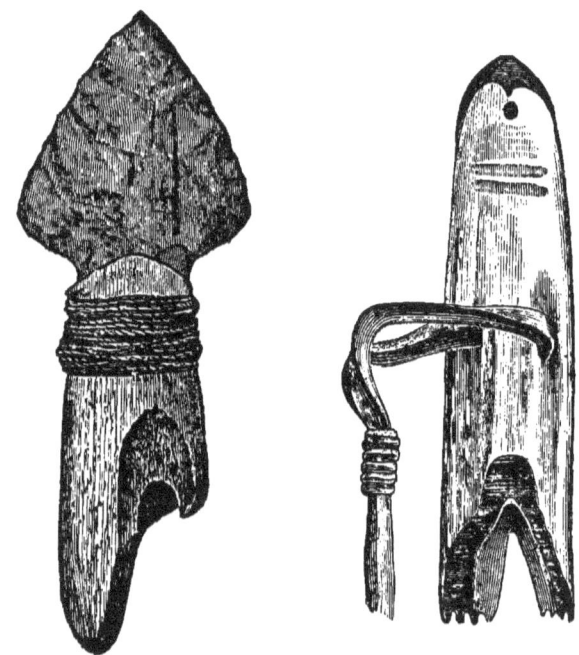

INNUIT HARPOON-HEADS.

better. Now God show his kindness to us; now he send his ministers to teach us the new way; now he building churches for us. Now we forsake the old way. We not like as we used to do—fight, shoot, wound, trouble, all the time. Now peace all the time. See my house—no ball or shot go through it.

All God's work now. Before the devil says to quarrel and fight and do bad ; now we have peace all the time ; nobody hurt us. [Bringing out his war-spear and defensive armor, and laying them in the middle of the room.] I fight no more. I give up my spear. All peace, all love now. I have a Saviour. He died on the cross to save me. I believe on God. I am now old. When I die I know where I go. I go to God, my Saviour. My heart is very happy now. I am in a bay where no wind ; no wind now to upset my canoe and trouble me. I am in a safe harbor. The Lord is my light and peace."

Toy-a-att was followed by John Kadeshan (also a chief), who said : " You have heard how bad I was long ago. I thought it good. When I do bad to any one I had a proud heart. I didn't know what I say or do. I do what the devil tell me. How great the change now. Some one whisper in my ear and humble my heart to God. Formerly white men come here and blind our hearts. They didn't tell us the way ; they learned us more badness. White men lie to us about other Indians, and make us enemies. We knew no God in heaven, and they didn't tell us. Then we hear a little about God at Fort Simpson and they tell us to pray God to send us a teacher, too. We then cry to God ; we ask God. He answer our prayers. He never forget us while sinners. He answer our prayer. He send Clah and Mrs. McFarland and Mr. Young. See how kind God is. He answer our poor prayer. We don't disbelieve God. See with your own eyes what God has done for us. Other Indians laugh at us because we cry to God for a teacher. But you see how it is. God heard. We no ashamed ; no disbelive him. White men laugh at us because we Christians. We don't care ; we not ashamed. They laugh against God, and cry down us. But we must strong our hearts, and not care for what they say.''

The next week Moses and Aaron, Matthew, Lot, Toy-a-att, Kadeshan, and the other Christian Indians combined and gave us a feast. It was held in Matthew's house. Previous to his conversion he had been a noted sorcerer, and his house was frequently used for the superstitious rites and devil-worship of heathenism. After his conversion it was as frequently used for church and school, by Clah. Upon my first visit to Fort Wrangell, to commence Presbyterian missions, I found upon the door the following :

NOTICE BY GOVERNOR MATTHEW.—That no Chinaman or white man allowed to have lodging in my house, only for Christ's service.
BY ORDER OF MATTHEW.
FORT WRANGELL, April 26, 1877.

At sunrise the boom of a cannon started us from our beds to look down the straits for an incoming steamer ; but it was a morning salute, fired by the Indians to express their joy that the day had come during which they could entertain those who had come all the way across from another ocean to see them. At noon another salute was fired, and boys sent through the village ringing hand-bells to announce that the feast was now ready. At one

ADOPTION INTO STICKEEN TRIBE.   109

o'clock we heard still another salute, which was the signal for us to start for the entertainment.

We were met at the door by chief Toy-a-att, decked in his official red shirt, dressed deer-skin leggins, and red, white and purple sash. He was followed by the leading men of the tribe, who met us with warm shaking of hands and boisterous expressions of delight. As Toy-a-att took the hand of Dr. Kendall, the booming cannon, ringing bells, and cheer upon cheer gave vent to the joy of assembled Indians at the presence of the great white chief of missions. Tables were arranged along two sides of the room, and covered with bread, crackers, cakes, pies, fish, corned beef, canned peaches, fresh berries, white sugar, butter, tea, coffee, etc. Two large bouquets of beautiful wild flowers added to the attractiveness of the tables. The chairs and seats were cushioned with blankets and costly furs. Upon a pole at the door waved the Stars and Stripes, and at the foot of the pole the small cannon used in firing the salute.

There were present eighteen whites and seventy-five Indians. During the dinner we were entertained with native music upon a tambourine drum. After dinner, of course speeches. Moses, rising from his seat, said :

"In our old ways, when a man succeeds to the chieftainship upon the death of his uncle he makes a great feast, and invites all the tribes far and near. For this he has been gathering blankets and furs and slaves for years. This feast lasts many days, during which the blankets and furs are given away, slaves killed and all the people fed. This entertainment will cost from $1000 to $2000 in presents and provisions. At this time the heir takes the name and place of the chief who is dead. His name costs him a great deal. We now honor you with the names of our people, without money or blankets. You, Dr. Kendall, whom we love, we name Kohan-ow (Cinnamon Bear, which kills lots of slaves), after my brother Aaron. And you, Dr. Jackson, we name Koostanine (Great Whale), for the whale family is influential among us. And you, Mrs Jackson, we call Ko-dā-te. And you, Dr. Corlies, we call San-to-nine (brother to Mr. Young). And you, Mr. Vanderbilt, we name Kadeshan."

Then Toy-a-att arose and said :

"I am sorry you sit in this old-fashioned Indian house. When you come back again we will have a new American house for you to sit in. But I am so happy you are here, I would not care if anybody kicked me. When we name our people we have a feast. We now give you our names and make you our people. Long ago I knew how to fight, and the people called me Toy-a-att (Great Fighter). I now give my name to Mr. Young, because he comes and fights our battles for us. And you, Dr. Lindsley, we call Tenn-na-take (Grandchild of Shaaks)."

After the speeches, some ballads narrating national history and traditions were sung. The tables were then cleared, and we had the tableau of a Chilcat princess in her royal dress.

The entertainment closed with the representation of a shaman healing the sick by sorcery. It was a

SHAMAN AND SICK MAN.

strange, weird scene. The sick man lay upon the floor in a blanket. Soon an Indian entered bearing upon his shoulder a large box, which was placed by the sick man. The box contained the paraphernalia of the sorcerer. The attendant was followed by the shaman dressed in the costume of his order, with long, dishevelled hair, rattles in his hand, and his face covered by a hideous mask. He walked around the fire in the centre of the room, occasionally casting side glances at the sick man and shaking his head dubiously. Soon a friend of the sick man brought in some furs and laid at the feet of the shaman, for he must have his pay in advance. He still shook his head, with low mutterings. More furs were brought, and again the friends went out and collected what they could to satisfy the shaman. When he had received all that the friends were able to gather, he commenced business.

Young men beat gongs and kept time with sticks on the floor, while the friends chanted a monotonous song. The shaman shook his rattles over the sick man and threw himself into every kind of hideous attitude, with horrible contortions of features. He rushed wildly around the fire, striking savagely at attendants with a dagger, flew at the sick man, ran his tongue at him, hissed, sometimes falling to the floor as if in a swoon. An attendant from time to time changed his mask and head-dress. Each mask represents a different spirit. And if one spirit has not sufficient power he tries another. Worked up to perfect frenzy, he finally declared that the sick man is bewitched, and immediately commences to trace up the witch. Hand over hand, as if following a cord in a labyrinth, or as a dog tracks his prey, he followed the imaginary line here and there until it ended at some person, who is accused of being the witch, and is often taken and tortured to death in order that the sick person, relieved from the baleful influence, may get well.

A few days later Shaaks, the head chief, gave the closing entertainment. Again we were greeted with booming cannons, ringing bells, and cheering Indians. The main representation at this time was the ancient potlach dance of the Tsimpseans.

There were eleven men and seven women among the performers. They were dressed in masks and costly robes and furs, representing a grizzly bear, a deer, porpoise, fox, crow, and other animals. It was a scene of barbaric gorgeousness that cannot well be described. At the conclusion of which Shaaks said :

"Dear brothers, this is how we used to do before white men came. We don't know who taught us these dances. But we liked them. Now, may God pity us, we so blind. All this we do long ago, but now it is past. God's word is never past. Now you see with your own eyes how blind we were. God don't like these things, and we put them away. Now we know better, and use them for the last time. God pity us, and send his Son to the world. White men knew it first. They pity us and tell us. Now you come to see us, and we are very happy."

CHAPTER III.

The Degradation of Indian Women in Alaska—Female Infanticide—The Sale of Girls—Female Slavery—Polygamy—Habitations of Cruelty—Widow-burning—Murder of the Old and Feeble

" Come and help us !" hear them calling,
Heathen in a Christian land,
Groaning under Satan's bondage,
Yearning for a helping hand."

As in all barbarous lands the heaviest burdens and greatest degradation fall upon the women, so in sections of Alaska.

From early childhood they are accustomed to every kind of drudgery and oppression.

Female infanticide is common among some of the tribes, particularly the Mahlemuts and those on the Yukon. Many Indian mothers, to save their daughters from their own wretched lives, take them out into the woods, stuff grass into their mouths, and leave them to die.

The Rev. W. W. Kirby, of the Church Missionary Society, who penetrated through British America to the Upper Yukon, says : " In common with all savage ᴘ ople, the Indians regard their women as slaves, and compel them to do the hardest work, while they look lazily on, enjoying the luxury of a pipe, and often requite their service with harsh words and cruel blows. They are inferior in looks and fewer in number than the men. The former probably arises from the harsh treatment they receive, and the latter is caused in a great measure by the too prevalent custom of female infanticide. Many a poor mother assured me that she had killed her child to save it from suffering the misery she had herself endured. . . . Then came the sad and harrowing tales of murder and infanticide. No fewer than thirteen women confessed to having slain their infant girls, some in the most cruel and heartless manner."

Spared in infancy, the lesson of inferiority is early burned into the lives of the girls. While mere babes they are sometimes given away or betrothed to their future husbands. And when they arrive at the age of twelve or fourteen years, among the Tinneh, the Thlinkets, and others, they are often offered for sale. For a few blankets a mother will sell her own daughter, for base purposes, for a week, a month, or for life.

All through that vast land wretched woman is systematically oppressed—made prematurely old in bearing man's burden as well as her own. In some sections all the work but hunting and fighting falls upon her—even the boys transferring their loads and work to their sisters.

Said a great chief, "Women are made to labor. One of them can haul as much as two men can do,

SLAVERY—POLYGAMY. 117

They pitch our tents, make and mend our clothing," etc.

And as if their ordinary condition was not bad enough, the majority of the slaves are women. The men captured in war are usually killed or reserved for torture, but the women are kept as beasts of burden, and often treated with great inhumanity. The master's power over them is unlimited. He can torture or put them to death at will. Sometimes, upon the death of the master, one or more of them are put to death, that he may have some one to wait upon him in the next world.

Polygamy, with all its attendant evils, is common among many tribes. These wives are often sisters. Sometimes a man's own mother or daughter is among his wives. If a man's wife bears him only daughters, he continues to take other wives until he has sons. One of the Nasse chiefs is said to have had forty wives.

On the Upper Yukon the man multiplies his wives as the farmer his oxen. The more wives, the more meat he can have hauled, the more wood cut, and more goods carried.

When a young girl arrives at maturity she is considered unclean. Everything she comes in contact with, and even the sky she looks upon, is considered unclean. She is therefore thought to be unfit for the sun to shine upon, and is confined for a year in a hut so small that she cannot stand upright in it. Only the girl's mother is allowed to approach her, and she only to bring her food.

Around Sitka this period has been shortened to three months. At the close of this imprisonment she is taken out, her old clothes burned, new ones provided, and a feast given, during which a slit is cut in the under lip, parallel with the mouth, and a piece of wood or shell inserted to keep the aperture extended. After marriage they are practically slaves of their husbands. Among some tribes their persons are at the disposal of visitors or travellers, guests of their husbands. They are sometimes, in Southern Alaska, sent to the mines, while the husband lives in idleness at home on the wages of their immorality. If ill-behaved, excessively lazy, or barren, they are sent away. Sometimes they are traded off by the husband for something he may desire. In childbirth, when needing the most tender care, they are driven out of the house as unclean, and kept for ten days in an uncomfortable hut, without attention. Their very lives are in his hands. During our visit to Fort Wrangell in 1879, an Indian killed his wife and brought her body into the village for a funeral. No one could interfere. According to their customs he had bought her as he would buy a dog, and if he chose he could kill her as he would kill a dog.

At the age of twelve to fourteen the girls are tortured with tattooing. According to Bancroft, " The color is applied by drawing a thread under the skin or pricking it in with a needle. The form varies among different tribes and different classes of the same tribe. The favorite colors seem to be red and blue, though black and leaden colors are common. A common woman of some of the tribes is permitted

TATTOOING.

to adorn her chin with but one vertical line in the centre and one parallel to it on either side, while a woman in the upper and wealthier classes is allowed two vertical lines from each corner of the mouth."

"Young Kadiak wives secure the affectionate admiration of their husbands by tattooing the breast and adorning the face with black lines, while the Kuskoquim women sew into their chins two parallel blue lines. And not content with tattooing, they also daub the face with various paints, make necklaces of copper wire, cover the face with grotesque wooden masks, scar their limbs and breasts with knives, pierce the nose, ears, and chin, filling the apertures with bones, shells, and pieces of copper, and attach heavy weights which draw the face out of proportion. The more the chin is riddled with holes the greater the respectability. Very aristocratic women sometimes have as many as six ornaments in their chin. They live in constant fear of innumerable spirits which fill the earth, the air, and the waters. Some of these spirits are good, but the majority of them are supposed to be evil and ever on the watch to do them harm. To appease the wrath of these evil spirits they employ the shamans to make offerings, and sometimes, though very rarely, offer a human sacrifice of a woman slave."

Among some Indians, on the Upper Yukon, when a man dies his widow is compelled to ascend the burning funeral-pile, throw herself upon the body, and remain there until the hair is burned from her head, and she is almost suffocated. She is then allowed to stagger from the pile, but must frequently thrust her hand through the flames and place it upon his bosom, to show her continued devotion. If through pain or faintness she fails to perform her duties, she is held up and pressed forward by others, her cries and shrieks being drowned in wild songs and the beating of drums. Finally, the ashes are gathered up and placed in a little sack, which the widow carries on her person for two years. During this period of mourning she is clothed in rags and treated as a slave. If there is more than one wife, they are ranged along the dead body of the husband, with their heads resting upon the corpse. This position is maintained until the hair is burned from their heads. When suffocated and almost senseless, they withdraw their heads from the fire, after which they hold one hand and then the other in the fire until the corpse is consumed. The ashes are gathered up and divided between them. Not unfrequently they commit suicide to avoid their slavery.

Among the Kariak the old and feeble are sometimes destroyed. This is done by placing a rope around the neck and dragging them over the stones. If this does not kill, then the body is stoned or speared and left to be eaten by the dogs. Occasionally the old ask to be killed. Then they are taken, stupefied with drugs, and, in the midst of various incantations, bled to death.

Among the Tuski and many of the tribes around the shores of Bering's Sea, the bodies of good men are burned and the ashes carefully preserved. But in some sections, where wood is scarce, the bodies of women are not considered worth the wood that would be consumed in the burning, and they are either cast out, to be consumed by the dogs, foxes, and crows, or cast into the sea as food for the fishes.

Despised by their fathers, sold by their mothers, imposed upon by their brothers, ill-treated by their husbands, cast out in their widowhood, living lives of toil and low sensual pleasure, untaught and uncared for, with no true enjoyment in this world and no hope for the world to come, crushed by a cruel heathenism, it is no wonder that many of them end their earthly misery and wretchedness with suicide.

In confirmation of the above dark picture, Captain Ebenezer Morgan, for many years the Christian captain of a whaling vessel in Alaska waters, at a large missionary meeting of ladies in New York City, made the following remarks :

" I have read all that my Brother Sheldon Jackson has published concerning Alaska, and I know of but one mistake he makes. *He does not say enough. He has not told you one half the degradation of those Northern Indians*, and I do not know where the suffering comes heavier than on the women, who are slaves and beasts of burden. *These pictures our brother has given are not strong enough. You would blush that the human family could be brought so low.*"

ESKIMO WOMAN AND BABE.

CHAPTER IV.

Greek and Lutheran Churches—Preliminary Steps Toward American Missions.

> " Lo ! to the wintry winds the pilot yields
> His bark careering o'er unfathomed fields ·
> Cold on his midnight watch the breezes blow
> From wastes that slumber in eternal snow,
> And waft across the waves' tumultuous roar
> *The wolf's long howl from Oonalaska's shore.*"
> CAMPBELL, *Pleasures of Hope.*

ON the 30th of June, 1793, the Empress Catharine of Russia issued an Imperial order that missionaries should be sent to her American colonies. In accordance with this order eleven monks sailed from Ochotsk for Kadiak Island, in charge of Archimandrite Joasaph, elder in the Order of Augustin Friars.

In 1796 Father Joasaph, being made bishop, returned to Irkutsk to receive consecration. The same year the first church building was erected at Kadiak.

In 1799 the newly-consecrated bishop and all the missionaries but one were shipwrecked and lost. This one monk remained alone in the colonies eleven years before another was sent to his assistance.

On December 5th, 1822, three more priests reached the colonies in safety.

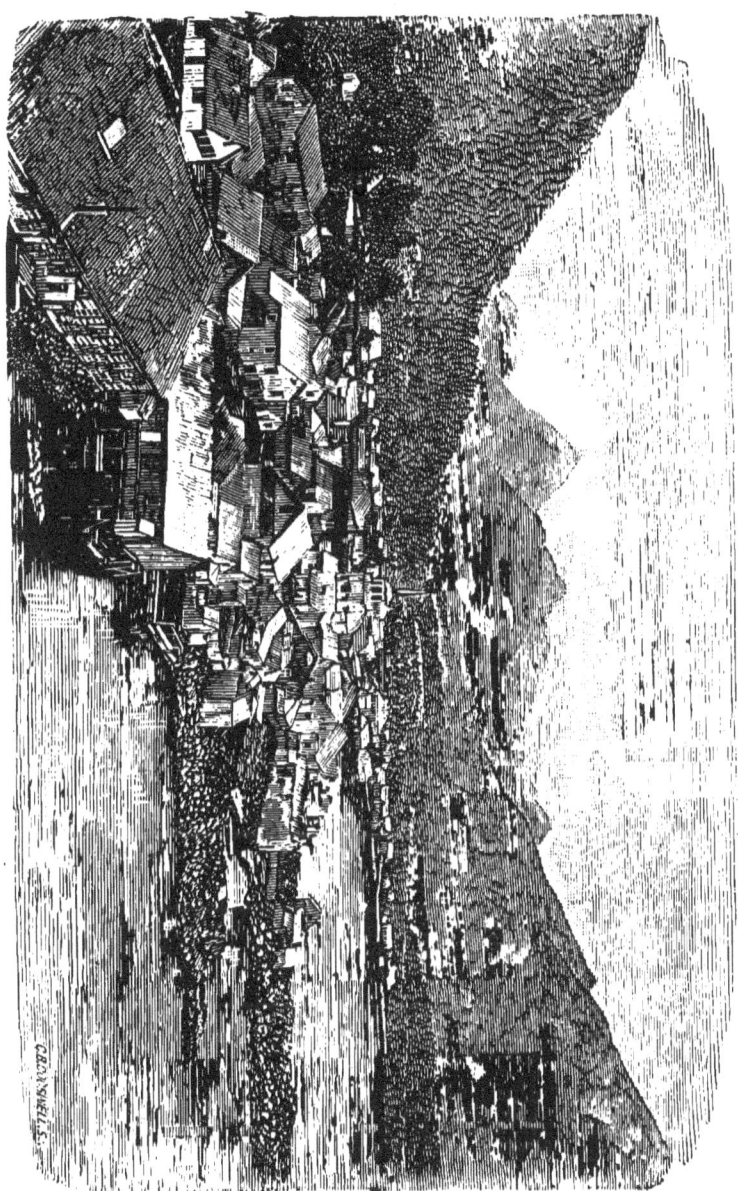

SITKA, ALASKA.

GREEK CHURCH—SCHOOLS. 127

But the one of all others to leave his impress upon the Aleuts was Innocentius Veniaminoff, who began his labors at Unalashka in 1823. In 1840 he was made bishop. He was subsequently advanced from one position to another until he was made Metropolite of Moscow, the highest position in the Greek Church. He died in the spring of 1879, mourned by a whole nation. He was the one among all the Russian priests to Alaska that has left an untarnished reputation and seemed to possess the true missionary spirit. At one time the Russian Greek Church had seven missionary districts in Alaska, with eleven priests and sixteen deacons; and in 1869 they claimed 12,140 members.

The Russian Fur Company contributed toward the support of the missions $6600 annually; $2313.75 was received from the Mission Fund of the Holy Synod, and $1100 from the sale of candles in the church, making about $10,000 annually. The balance came from private individuals. From these revenues the mission churches had accumulated, up to 1860, a surplus of $37,500, which was loaned out at five per cent.

The first school was established by Shelikoff on the Island of Kadiak, the pupils receiving instruction in the Russian language, arithmetic, and religion. This was about 1792. A few years later one was established in Sitka. In 1841 an ecclesiastical school was opened in Sitka, which in 1845 was raised to the rank of a seminary.

But little was taught in the schools but the rites of

the Greek Church and the art of reading the ecclesiastical characters.

In 1860 a colonial school was opened, with twelve students. In 1862 it contained twenty-seven students, only one of whom was a native.

In 1839 a girls' school was established for orphans and children of the employés of the Fur Company ; in 1862 it had twenty-two pupils. In 1825 a school was established on Unalaska Island for natives ; in 1860 it had thirty boys and forty-three girls. A school at Amlia Island in 1860 had thirty pupils. A schoolhouse was built on the Lower Yukon, but had no pupils.

Since the American occupation these schools have been suspended.

During the Russian domination there were many Swedes, Finlanders, and Germans in the employ of the Russian American Fur Company.

To provide for this population a Lutheran minister was sent to Sitka in 1845 and remained until 1852. He was succeeded by Rev. Mr. Wintec, who preached in Swedish and German. He remained until the transfer in 1867, when, his support being withdrawn by the Russian Government, he returned to Europe.

The Protestant churches of Russia, while allowed no self-governing and self-sustaining organizations, are recognized under the Ministerium of Public Instruction. They have a consistorium for each province, and the funds for salaries, etc., come direct from the public treasury.

While the Lutheran minister remained at Sitka, a

fund of several thousand dollars was accumulated for furnishing the church, etc.

No organization was made, and the cause dropped out of sight upon the final removal of the minister.

When in 1867 this vast territory, with a population of from 30,000 to 50,000 souls, was turned over to the United States, the call of God's providence came to the American church to enter in and possess the land for Christ.

And in response to that call it was to be expected that the churches of the United States, with their purer religion and greater consecration, would send in more efficient agencies than Russia had done. But ten years rolled around, and the churches did nothing. Ten years passed, and hundreds of immortal souls, who have never so much as heard that there was a Saviour, were hurried to judgment from a Christian land. Ten years came and went, and thousands were left to grow up in ignorance and superstition, and form habits that will keep them away from the gospel, if it is ever offered them.

It was also to be expected that the great missionary societies of the country would vie with one another which should first unfurl the banner of the Gospel in that land, but for years nothing was done, and yet the question was not wholly lost sight of. It was more or less agitated by various persons in different denominations and widely separated sections of the country.

Among others, the Rev. E. D. Saunders, D.D., of the Board of Domestic Missions of the Presbyterian Church (O. S.), soon after the purchase, offered a

130 MISSIONS PROPOSED.

resolution in his board that they send a missionary to Alaska.

At the same time a similar proposition was discussed by the Committee of Home Missions of the Presbyterian Church (N. S.).

At different times, from 1869 to 1877, the Rev. George H. Atkinson, D.D., Superintendent of Congregational Missions in the North-west, urged the Mission Board of his denomination to undertake the work.

Major General O. O. Howard, U. S. A., again and again pressed the religious needs of that section upon the attention of the country through the newspapers.

The Hon. Vincent Colyer, Secretary of the Board of Indian Commissioners, made a special visit to Alaska in 1869, and upon his return sought to awaken the public interest. He so far succeeded that Congress appropriated $50,000 for educational purposes. But no one was found to administer the fund, and it was not used.

On my long stage trips, while establishing churches thoughout the Rocky Mountain Territories, I had often thought of that distant section of our country, and the vague hope would sometimes cross my mind that I myself might yet be permitted to go there. I could not then anticipate the unexpected providences by which afterward I became the first Presbyterian minister to visit Alaska in the interest of missions and commence the work of the Presbyterian Church.

I had also, during the winter of 1875 and 1876, in view of the approaching Centennial, urged upon the

MISSIONS URGED. 131

Board of Home Missions the desirability of so extending their work that the Presbyterian Church could celebrate the completion of the first century of our national existence with missionaries in every State and Territory, calling special attention to Arizona, Dakota, and Alaska.

To assist in accomplishing this, I made a long and dangerous trip through Arizona in the spring of 1876, which resulted in sending two ministers to that Territory.

During 1876 the Rev. Thomas Crosby, of the Methodist Church of Canada, stationed at Fort Simpson, B. C., was in active correspondence with the Board of Missions of his own church, also with that of the Methodist Episcopal Church of the United States, and with one of the Presbyterian Churches of Canada, pleading with them to secure missionaries for Alaska.

The Rev. A. L. Lindsley, D.D., corresponded with the Presbyterian Board of Foreign Missions, in 1877, with reference to their undertaking the work.

In the spring of that year, through Major-General Howard, he secured the position of paymaster's clerk in the United States Army for Mr. John C. Mallory, of New York City (who was passing through Portland in search of health and a position), and had him sent north to ascertain and report the condition of affairs. Mr. Mallory was, however, so far gone with consumption that he returned in a few weeks and accepted an Indian agency in Arizona, where he died the 20th of June, 1878.

Christian women, wives of the army officers stationed at Sitka and Wrangell, were continually writing to their friends concerning the need of missionaries.

Probably there were many others interested in Alaska.

But notwithstanding all these movements, the churches slept and mission boards waited. Not so, however, with God's providence : it never waits.

In the spring of 1876 Clah (Philip McKay), Sugah-na-te (his brother), Ta-lik, John Ryan, Lewis Ween, Andrew Moss, Peter Pollard, George Pemberton, and James Ross, Tsimpsean Indians, went from Fort Simpson to Fort Wrangell to obtain work. They secured a contract to cut wood for the Government. On Sabbath, as was their custom, they met together for worship. This gathering of a few Christian Indians was the commencement of missions in the Territory.

They found a protector and warm friend in Captain S. P. Jocelyn, of the 21st U. S. Infantry, who was then in command at that station. He assisted them in securing a room for worship on the Sabbath, and protected them from interruption.

He also supplied them with some small hymnbooks that had been sent to the fort by the American Tract Society.

In September of that year Rev. Thomas Crosby visited Fort Wrangell and held services. The Presbyterian Church owes much to him for his unselfish zeal and assistance at a critical period in the history of the mission.

With the assistance of Captain Jocelyn, Mr. Crosby

SUBSCRIPTION FOR A CHURCH. 133

held a meeting of whites and Indians to take measures toward securing a church and school building. There was a good deal of enthusiasm, and the Indians made the following subscription :

Tribe.	Name.	Amount.
Stickeen.	Chief Toy-a-att....................	$10 00
"	Jun Lewy........................	5 00
"	Mrs. Lewy.......................	5 00
"	Miss Lewy......................	5 00
"	Lewy's two children..............	5 00
"	Charley and wife, two blankets, white and green.	
"	Dick, one blanket, white.	
"	Thos. Steele, one blanket, white.	
"	Jennie.........................	5 00
"	Jennie's two children............	5 00
"	Mary...........................	10 00
"	Billy...........................	50
"	Dan............................	50
"	Sarah, two blankets, blue and green.	
"	Susan..........................	1 00
"	Jack............................	50
"	George Blake...................	2 00
"	Billy Lewy......................	2 00
Cassiar.	George	5 00
"	George's wife...................	5 00
"	George's boy Sam...............	5 00
"	Paul Jones, Jr.	50
Tarko.	Pat.............................	50
Hydah.	John...........................	1 00
Tsimpseans.	Harry..........................	1 00
"	Louis...........................	1 00
"	Thomas........................	1 00
"	George.........................	1 00
"	Moss...........................	1 00
"	Shaw...........................	1 00

SUBSCRIPTION FOR A CHURCH.

Tribe.	Name.	Amount.
Tsimpseans.	Philip	$1 00
"	Nelly Miller	50
"	William Dickinson	25
Clawock.	George	50
"	Mary Ann	1 50
"	Sarah M. Dickinson	25
Sitka.	Kate,	1 00
"	William Stephens, Jr.	50

HOUSE OF THE WIDOW OF SKILLAT, THE FORMER CHIEF, AT WRANGELL, ALASKA.

In addition to the money and blankets, they also agreed to do much of the work.

Mr. I. C. Dennis, the Collector of the Port, consented to act as treasurer. He afterward turned over the funds to Mr. J. M. Vanderbilt, who in turn gave them to Rev. Mr. Young for the Presbyterian Church in 1879.

SCHOOL AND PREACHING. 135

Mr. Crosby agreed to look after the mission until some American missionary should come and assume the control.

Accordingly, when the young men at the close of their contract in the fall would return to Fort Simpson, he directed Clah to remain and open a day school and conduct the Sabbath services. Lewis Ween and George Pemberton secured positions at Wrangell and assisted Clah on the Sabbath. So anxious were the natives to learn, that the school was attended by sixty or seventy adults. And three times on the Sabbath he preached to audiences of from 200 to 400 of his own people. This subjected these Tsimpsean Christians to much ridicule from the Americans, and threats of violence from the Indian sorcerers. But they persevered, and the meetings increased in interest and numbers. A few Americans attended to ridicule, but more were attracted by the sight of unlettered Indians singing, praying, and explaining the Scriptures with power. Prayerless white men were reminded of early religious training. The Holy Spirit was at work among the natives, and forty of them gave up their heathenism and came out upon the Lord's side, while many others renounced their devil dances, their witchcraft, and other heathen practices.

A soldier at the post, not himself a Christian, wrote the following letter to Major-General Howard, asking that some church might be persuaded to send a minister to guide this movement and teach these new converts more perfectly the way :

"DEAR SIR : I write you in behalf of the Indians in this section of Alaska, hoping that you may be able and willing to assist these poor creatures in their endeavors to learn more of the good Saviour, of whom they have learned but recently.

"About last June a party of Indians from Fort Simpson, British Columbia, arrived at Wrangell and instituted a series of meetings for divine worship. The Stickeens and other tribes here really knew nothing about Christianity. They soon became interested in the proceedings of their Christian visitors, and a few, after many inquiries, concluded to try the ' new life ' of which they had heard. Since then the few have become a hundred, and the tribe are asking for a Christian teacher, for some one to explain to them more fully the way.

"Rev. Mr. Crosby, of Fort Simpson, came here last fall and did noble work for a few days, but his own mission demanded his presence, and he could only leave two young men (Indians) of his church to continue the work. It has been manfully carried on during the winter, and could you, gentlemen, be present during some of their services, I know your hearts would go out to them at the earnestness of their prayers and their intense mental struggles between the prejudices of their tribal teachings and the new doctrines of Christianity. They are poor financially, and while their country is unfitted for anything like agriculture, the waters are rich in fish, and the land full of game and heavily covered with timber. Since the advent of traders and miners among them, lewdness and debauchery have held high carnival, and the decimation of their numbers is the result. If a school and mission were established at Wrangell there would no doubt an Indian population of over 1000 souls locate within reach of its benefits. And one whole-souled, energetic worker here could sow seed that would bear fruit from British Columbia to Bering's Straits.

"These Indians have patriotic ideas, are proud to call themselves 'Boston Siwashes' (United States Indians), and glory in the possession of a 'star-spangled banner.' But they feel bad when they learn how much better off than themselves are the Indians of British Columbia. Schools and churches abound among the British Indians, so that nearly all of them can read and write, and appear to better advantage than their neighbors in Alaska. This fact speaks much for the Christian people of Canada, and little for those of our own Republic, who yearly send so much to convert the heathen in other lands, while they allow our own countrymen, who certainly are just as deserving, to go down to the lowest hell.

"I am not a church member, but am making this appeal for these poor people from the dictates of a heart that I trust may never be deaf to the cry for help from the heathen. Can you not, will you not, make it your business to build up and foster this mission to Alaska? A number of men could be employed advantageously, but one whole-souled man can do much and pave the way for doing more. Send out a shepherd who may reclaim a mighty flock from the error of their ways and gather them to the true fold, the Master of which said: 'Feed my sheep.' I hope that this letter may be considered in all charity, blemishes excluded.

"And now, with faith in the justness of the cause for which I plead so feebly, I leave the matter in your hands, trusting that a brighter day may soon dawn for the poor benighted natives of Alaska.

"Yours sincerely,

This letter was placed in my hands at the General Assembly of 1877 at Chicago. I immediately published it in the Chicago *Tribune*, and soon after in the leading Presbyterian newspapers. I also sent a copy to the Board of Home Missions, with an urgent appeal for action.

The board responded at its first meeting (June, 1877) by appointing Rev. Francis H. Robinson as missionary to Alaska, but before he received his commission he had accepted an invitation to a church in California.

Returning from the General Assembly, I was sent by the secretaries of the Board of Home Missions on a special mission tour through Idaho, Eastern Oregon, and Eastern Washington. Arriving at Walla Walla, I found the whole section agitated by the outbreak of Chief Joseph's band of Nez Perces, and the exposed settlers fleeing from their homes. This condition of things was so unfavorable to mission work that I was able to extend my trip to Alaska.

Upon reaching Portland and consulting with Dr. Lindsley and other ministers of that section, my purpose to visit Alaska was warmly approved.

MRS. MCFARLAND. 139

I also found at Portland an old missionary friend, Mrs. A. R. McFarland, who was waiting my arrival to consult with regard to future work.

Born in Virginia, Mrs. McFarland was educated at Steubenville, Ohio. Upon her marriage she accompanied her husband to Illinois, where they spent ten years in home mission work. In 1867 they were sent to Santa Fé, New Mexico, the first Presbyterian missionaries to that Territory.

While in that field she crossed the plains from the Missouri River to Santa Fé in a stage-coach several times. Upon one occasion, for twelve days and nights she was the only woman in the coach, and a portion of the way they were pursued by the wild Indians of the plains. Through many dangers and trials she has been prepared for frontier work.

In 1873 they went to Southern California for Mr. McFarland's health. This improving, and wishing to re-enter the mission field, they accepted positions among the Nez Perces in 1875. Hard work and a severe climate again laid Mr. McFarland aside, and in May, 1876, he laid down the cross to take up his crown. Unable to endure the feeling of desolation and loneliness, Mrs. McFarland, in January, 1877, removed to Portland, Oregon. But her missionary spirit could not be satisfied there, and she was waiting with prayerful anxiety my arrival to apply for a new field.

It was soon determined that she should accompany me to Alaska.

CHAPTER V.

The Commencement of Presbyterian Missions in Alaska—Mrs. A. R. McFarland—Her Varied Duties—Sickness and Death of Clah—Christmas Welcome.

> " Shores of the utmost West,
> Ye that have waited long,
> Unvisited, unblest,
> Break forth to swelling song ;
> High raise the note that Jesus died,
> Yet lives and reigns the Crucified."

ON the 10th of August, 1877, Mrs. McFarland and myself reached Fort Wrangel and commenced Presbyterian missions in Alaska.

Upon landing and passing down the street, I saw an Indian ringing a bell. It was the call for the afternoon school. About twenty pupils were in attendance, mostly young Indian women. Two or three boys were present ; also a mother and her three little children. As the women took their seats on the rough plank benches, each one bowed her head in silent prayer, seeking divine help on her studies. Soon a thoughtful Indian man of about thirty years of age came in and took his seat behind the rude desk. It was Clah, the teacher. The familiar hymn, " What a friend we have in Jesus," was sung in English ;

PRESBYTERIAN CHURCH—THE McFARLAND INDUSTRIAL HOME AND VILLAGE OF FORT WRANGELL, ALASKA.

INDIAN SCHOOL. 143

a prayer followed in the Chinook jargon,* closing with the repetition in concert of the Lord's Prayer in English. After lessons were studied and recited, the school arose, sung the long-metre doxology, and recited in concert the benediction. Then the teacher said, "Good afternoon, my pupils," to which came the kindly response, "Good afternoon, teacher."

As upon the Sandwich Islands, and more lately in Old Mexico, so here God had opened the work in advance of the coming of the usual missionary appliances.

The mission school was in full operation, but under great difficulties.

They met around in the several Indian houses, not always knowing one day where they would meet the next. But the ringing of a small hand-bell indicated the school-room for the day. At the time of my visit they were using a dance-hall. Upon the return of the miners in the fall the school was turned out of the hall and found refuge in an old log building.

There was a great scarcity of school-books and appliances. I found the stock inventoried as follows : Four small Bibles, four hymn-books, three primers, thirteen first readers, and one wall chart. "These people," remarked a sailor, "are crazy to learn. Going up the beach last night I heard an Indian girl spelling words of one and two syllables. Looking in I found that, unable to procure a school-

* Chinook jargon is a language composed of French, Canadian, English, and Indian words, and was used by the Hudson Bay Fur Company in their trade with the various Indian tribes. A Chinook and English dictionary has been published.

book, she was learning from a scrap of newspaper she had picked up."

Arranging for the work, I returned to the East, leaving Mrs. McFarland in charge as teacher and Clah as native assistant teacher, and Mrs. Sarah Dickinson, a Christian Tongas Indian, as interpreter. When we reached Wrangel this woman was a hundred miles up the Stickeen River gathering her winter supply of berries. Learning from a passing steamer that the missionaries had come, she placed her children, bedding, and provisions in her canoe, and paddled home, against heavy head winds, to give us a welcome.

During that fall and winter I published a lengthy series of newspaper articles and made public addresses in New York City, Philadelphia, Washington, and the other principal cities of the North, creating such an interest in Alaska that special funds have been sent in, from October, 1877, to December, 1879, aggregating over $12,000. This enabled the Board of Home Missions to carry on the work in that section without drawing from the general missionary treasury.

I also addressed the students at the theological seminaries, and secured the appointment, by the Board of Home Missions, of Rev. John G. Brady, of Union Theological Seminary, for Sitka, Alaska; Rev. S. Hall Young, of Allegheny Theological Seminary, for Fort Wrangell, and Rev. George W. Gallagher, of Princeton Theological Seminary. Mr. Gallagher was afterward transferred to the Utah field.

MRS. A. R. MCFARLAND.

A REMARKABLE WOMAN. 147

Later I secured the appointment of Miss Maggie J. Dunbar, of Steubenville, Ohio, as teacher at Fort Wrangell, and still later that of Rev. G. W. Lyons, who was commissioned by the board in January, 1880, for Sitka.

During the same winter I had a hearing before several committees of Congress in behalf of a government for Alaska.

Mrs. McFarland entered upon her work with great earnestness and wisdom. Her matured Christian experience and her eventful life on the frontier had eminently prepared her for the responsible and wonderful work she was now entering upon. It will be borne in mind at that time she was the only Christian white woman in Wrangell, that she was for seven months the only Protestant missionary in Alaska, and for twelve months the only one at Fort Wrangell.

It will also be noticed that all the perplexities, political, religious, physical, and moral, of the native population were brought to her for solution, and that her arbitration was universally accepted. If any were sick, they came to her as a physician; if any were dead, she was called upon to take charge of the funeral. If husbands and wives became separated, she was the peacemaker to settle their difficulties. If difficulties arose as to property, she was judge, lawyer, and jury. If feuds arose among the small tribes or families, she was arbiter. And when the Christian Indians called a constitutional convention, she was elected chairman. She was called upon to interfere in cases of witchcraft; and when the Vigilance Committee would hang a white man for murder, she was sent for to act as his spiritual adviser. Her fame also went out far and wide among the tribes. Great chiefs left their homes and people and came long distances to enter the school of "the woman that loved their people," or to plead that teachers might be sent to their tribes. She had charge of both school and church./ During this trying period she was greatly assisted by the counsel and substantial aid of Mr. John M. Vanderbilt, the leading merchant, and Mr. I. C. Dennis, Collector of the Port.

The history of her work cannot better be made known than by giving her monthly letters to the Rocky Mountain *Presbyterian*, an illustrated Home Missionary journal.

"FORT WRANGELL, ALASKA, Sept. 10th, 1877.

"REV. SHELDON JACKSON, D.D.

"DEAR BROTHER: I went into the school-room the morning after you left, and have become very much interested in the school. It now averages thirty scholars. I have had as high as thirty-eight some days. They all seem very anxious to learn. Clah studies in the forenoon. He and Mrs. Dickinson are in a class together. They study reading, spelling, geography, and writing. I go at nine o'clock and remain until one. Then Clah has a short session in the afternoon. I am teaching the whole school the multiplication table in unison. Clah is much pleased to learn it. They have gotten the second and third lines perfectly. Since Mrs.

THE McFARLAND SCHOOL, FORT WRANGELL, ALASKA, 1877.

Dickinson came home, Clah preaches in Tsimpsean, and Mrs. D. interprets his sermon into Stickeen.

"He preaches with much more ease in Chinook than he does in his own language, but it seems that many of the old people do not understand the Chinook.

"Clah's wife came up on the steamer. She is quite good-looking, rather dignified and reserved. She does not speak a word of English. He seems quite proud of her.

"Two weeks ago last Saturday I was sent for to see a sick man. He belonged to the Hydah tribe, and was thought to be dying, having just had a severe hemorrhage. No wonder he felt like dying. Upon reaching the house I found sixty-five people in the room, with a big fire in the centre. I asked him, through the interpreter, if I could do anything for him. He replied that he wanted me to pray for him, and when he died that I would see him buried like a white man. He said that he had heard of Jesus Christ, and that he believed in him. At another visit he urged me to teach all Indians to pray. He wanted me to sing. I sang 'There is a fountain filled with blood,' and endeavored to explain the meaning of the words to him. In a few days he was better, and his friends took him home. I do not know whether they will carry out his wish for a Christian burial. Several chiefs have been to see me. They are all very anxious to have a 'white man preacher come,' and to have a 'church house like Fort Simpson' (the mission station of the Methodists in British Columbia).

"Last week I had a prominent chief of the Takou tribe to see me. He seemed to be a very sensible man, and expressed great anxiety to have a school for his people.

"Our school-room has been rented for a dance-house, and will be taken from us by the 15th of the month. I went to see the house that belonged to Matthew, but it would not answer. I have since secured an old log house, which the owner has agreed to repair and rent us for $20 per month. I have rented the little house back of Mr. Lear's store to live in. It was the very best I could do.

"I am exceedingly anxious to have a room furnished as soon as possible, where I can take any young girls that may have a disposition to do right. Such an one recently came and wanted to stay with me. She was bright and smart, and talked English well, but I was not so situated that I could take her. When I next heard of her she was living with a white man. I hope I will have sufficient aid to offer a home to such cases when they present themselves. I believe I could have saved that girl if I could have offered her a home. Yours truly,

"A. R. McFarland."

"Fort Wrangell, Alaska, Oct. 11th, 1877.

"Dear Brother: I rejoice to write that I am now moved and in my own house. I find this little house very comfortable—much more so than seemed possible, with so little to fix it with. The people have been very kind in helping me move.

"Clah has moved into Matthew's house. His wife

comes to school now. I was surprised to find that she does not know her A B C's. I asked Clah how long they had been married. He replied, ' My father gave me Annie when I was a little boy, for a present, and I have lived with her ever since.' Matthew comes to school, and is very anxious to learn. He says, ' Me want to learn quick, so me can read the Bible all the time.' I had a funny experience with him last week. He and his wife had quarrelled, and had not lived together for almost a year. She is one of my best scholars, and I saw that she was in great trouble. I found she wanted to go back to her husband. So I brought Matthew home with me one day and had a long talk with him. He said that he and his wife had lived together very happily for ten years. But last fall some people told him that she was a bad woman, and that if he was a Christian he ought not to live with her. I answered him, that although his wife may have done some wrong things, yet if he was a Christian he ought to forgive her—that he had no right to ask God to forgive him if he could not forgive his wife. He went away very thoughtful. The next day he came back in great trouble, saying he had not been able to sleep all night. He wanted me to see his wife. So I appointed a meeting for the next day, when we would all be present; also another man and wife who had come to me with their troubles. The two couples came at the appointed time. I had Clah and Mrs. Dickinson present. I made it a religious meeting, and as solemn as possible. After each one had told their grievances, I summed up with the necessity of mutual forbearance—that they should forgive one another, try to be happy together, and live as Christians should. This they agreed to, and went away satisfied, and are seemingly doing well since. This is new work for me.

"I do hope that we shall get a minister soon to attend to such cases as this. I do not know that I am very wise about some things, but I try to do the best I can, seeking help from above. There is a very aggravated case here of one of our schoolgirls. If I can get her away I will bring her to my house. Pray for me that I may have wisdom to do what is right about all these things. I hope there may be money furnished me from some source to offer a home in such cases, where it may seem wise to do so.

"We now hold the school in the old log house, but it is too small and cold. I had to purchase the lumber for the seats.

"The Roman Catholics had sent to Europe for a priest for this place, so that if I had not come when I did they would have had the field. They expected to have commenced this fall. There has a little leaven of Catholicism already crept in. I have had to remonstrate with some of them about the confessional."

"October 15th, 1877.

"I have very sad news to write. Our dear Clah is very sick—nigh unto death. Night before last an Indian came after me, saying that Clah was dying and wanted to see me right away. I dressed and went as quickly as I could, and found that he had

THE SEWING-SCHOOL. 155

been suddenly taken with a severe hemorrhage. I feared that he would not live until morning. To-day he seems better, but has bad symptoms. I asked him that first night whether he was willing to go if it should be the Lord's will. He replied that he would like to have seen a minister here first, but that it was all right. The Indians are very much distressed about his being sick."

"October 19.

"Clah has had no return of the bleeding, but is very feeble, and to-day I find his hands and feet swollen very much. I also found Mrs. Dickinson very sick in bed with a severe cold. So you see how full my hands are.

"There have been three young men here from Fort Simpson attending school. One of them is a preacher, but he can only preach in his own language, and now that Mrs. Dickinson is sick and there is no one to interpret for him, I do not know how we shall get along.

"The Indians came flocking in yesterday upon the arrival of the steamer to know whether there was 'any word about a white man preacher coming.'

"The women and girls come to my house three afternoons in the week for a sewing-school. This, with being in day-school, visiting the sick, and attending to my household duties, keeps me very busy.

"Yours truly,   A. R. McFarland."

"Fort Wrangell, Alaska, Nov. 10th, 1877.

"Dear Brother: My hands are so full, and I feel so exhausted when evening comes, that it is an effort for me to write. Clah is still sick, but seems to be improving slowly. He looks very badly, but is quite cheerful. I asked him if he did not feel more encouraged about getting well. He said, 'I don't know. If Jesus makes my wind strong, all right. Me get up and preach. Jesus make my wind (breath) stop, all right, me die.'

"I have three other sick ones on my hands. The boys from Fort Simpson have all gone home but one. I kept Andrew to do the preaching until Clah gets better. I feel so anxious for a minister to come for many reasons. One is, there are some young Indians here who wish very much to get married. I am also hopeful that some of the white men would marry the girls they are living with if there was a minister here. And it will make a great change for the better.

"I had a letter from Mr. Crosby, sending the church certificate of Clah and his wife and expressing a great deal of interest in the work here. Mrs. Dickinson, my interpreter, continues very zealous and faithful.

"I had a Hydah man come into my school today. He looks to be about forty-five years old. He says he came here to go to school, so that he can go back and teach his own people. He did not know the first letter of the alphabet. Yesterday a chief by the name of Hotchcox came to school. He said he was from Buffalo Island, and wanted to talk with me. He was a remarkably fine-looking man, and I felt that if the Christians of the East who have abundant means, could have seen him with the tears running down his face, and heard what he said, there would be no lack of money to carry on the work in Alaska. Laying his hand upon his heart, he says, ' Me much sick heart. You come teach all Stickeens, all Hydahs, all Tongas about God. My people all dark heart. Nobody tell them that Jesus died. By and bye all my people die (pointing down), go down, down, dark.' He was completely overcome. Oh, how my heart ached. I tried to comfort him by telling him that we hoped to be able to send preachers and teachers to all these people soon.

"My sewing-school is getting along nicely, and I hope will be productive of much good. The women and girls are delighted with coming to my house to work, and to have me assist them with their sewing. We take a verse of Scripture, and while at work they memorize it, and I try to make them understand its meaning. I try to give them the right ideas about a great many other things. Then we close with singing and prayer. I would be glad if there was some person to take the school off my hands that I might devote my whole time to this kind of work. You know how much need there is of it. As I am now situated, I cannot attend to the sick as I would like. I think I am a very strong woman (physically), yet I have realized many times of late that I am not made of iron. Mr. and Mrs. Vanderbilt are very kind to me indeed.

"Since writing the above there has been an occurrence which, while it does not amount to much in itself, yet has made some excitement among this superstitious people. It seems that a young Indian by the name of Johnson went with his father some distance to cut wood. While encamped there he had a wonderful dream. Upon his return he narrated the dream at an evening meeting. He dreamed that he died and went to heaven. He stood at the side of the gate and saw all the school Indians come up. The keeper allowed some of them to pass in, but others were kept out. He said that they were good people, but that they had been living in sin—because they had never been married to those with whom they were living. There was much more to his dream, and it has created great consternation. A number who have had no opportunity of getting married after the American way are very much troubled, and are more anxious that a minister may come quickly, who can marry them.

"Yours truly, A. R. McFARLAND."

On Friday, December 28th, 1877, Clah, whose English name was Philip McKay, died with consumption, aged thirty years. When the preaching of the Gospel was commenced among the Tsimpseans at Fort Simpson, by some converted Indians from Victoria, Clah was among the first to believe and be baptized. Giving himself faithfully to the study of the Bible and the advantages of the mission school, he made such rapid advances that he was stationed at Wrangell in 1876.

Upon my first visit he was teaching the day-school six days in the week, holding prayer-meetings Tuesday and Friday evenings, and preaching three times on the Sabbath. Though not understanding a word

CLAH (PHILIP McKAY).

of his sermons, yet I was greatly impressed with his earnest and yet dignified and easy delivery in preaching. During his first year in preaching he mostly lived on fish. Fish for breakfast, dinner and supper, month after month ; and now and then, when fresh fish was scarce, he had smoked fish for a change. His salary of $10 a month would not admit of any luxuries.

His body was taken to Fort Simpson and buried in the Christian Indian cemetery, which I visited in the fall of 1879, in company with Rev. Thomas Crosby. It crowns a beautiful hill overlooking the bay.

Passing by the crest-poles, in which, formerly, with heathen rites, they deposited the ashes of the cremated dead, we came to a cemetery laid out in modern style, many of the graves being adorned with marble headstones and covered with flowers. Among the inscriptions were the following :

"His end was peace." "There is hope in his death." "Jesus pity me. Take my hand and lead me to the Father. I have been poor in the world, and wicked. But all is over now. Take me home to God." "Said to his father, trust in God." "He departed trusting in Jesus." "Of such is the kingdom of Heaven." Upon the stone of a chief who was drowned by the splitting of his canoe, "His last act was to sing a hymn and offer prayer to God."

The following was Clah's last letter :

"FORT WRANGELL, Sept. 14, 1877.

"DR. JACKSON.

"RESPECTED SIR : We are getting along nicely since you left. Mrs. McFarland gives us all good satisfaction ; in fact, we are all pleased with her. I keep up the meetings three times on Sabbath, and Tuesdays and Fridays. Our members are doing very well. No doubt Mrs. McFarland will write you all the particulars. My wife has come up from Fort Simpson, and I shall need a house to live in. I do not know what I shall do, as I shall not have money enough to live with and expend any on a house. Neither can I pay rent with my salary, and keep even. I had only $28 or $30 on which to live from the time you left to the 1st of October, and if this has to be taken from my pay after the 1st of October, it will make me awful short. If I could start even on the 1st of October I could get along splendid, if I had a small room to live in. We expected to hear from you by return steamer, but were disappointed. We want your prayers to God for our success in converting these Indians. It is my constant prayer to God that these Indians may all be made to know Christ, and we earnestly ask that all the churches will pray for us, as we need all your prayers to God. Yours very respectfully,

"PHILIP McKAY."

Soon after Clah's death, Mrs. McFarland wrote :

'FORT WRANGELL, ALASKA, Jan. 16th, 1878.

" DR. JACKSON.

" DEAR BROTHER : Although we have commenced a new year, we feel sadly broken up and discouraged, for God has taken away our beloved Philip. He passed away very peacefully, on Friday, December 28th, 1877.

THE DEATH OF CLAH.

"I went up to see him on Thursday. He talked very cheerfully. Said he thought he had only a few hours to live. I asked him how death seemed to him. He replied, 'As earth fades away, heaven grows brighter.' His wife was crouched down by his bed weeping. He turned to her and said, 'Annie, you must not cry; Jesus knows what is best.'

"His friends took his body to Fort Simpson to bury it beside his mother and three brothers, who were drowned last summer.

"The natives raised sufficient money among themselves to pay for the coffin and build a fence around his grave. I think it was very thoughtful in them. Philip's dying request was that the Christian friends in the East should do something for his wife. He said, 'My wife and little boy will be left without anything to buy food with, and it troubles me.' I told him he must not worry about it, that the Lord would raise up friends for them; and asked him if he could not leave them in the Lord's hands? He replied that he would try and trust all to Jesus.

"My school is very full, and I am about as busy as it is possible for a person to be. Oh! I do pray that the Lord will soon send us help.

"There is a good deal of alarm among the Christian natives about the Catholics. Word has come from Victoria that two priests are coming here to build a church. Shus-taks, the rich chief you went to see, is very anxious to have them come, and has promised them much help in building a church.

"I am rejoiced to report that we are moved back with the school and church into the dance-house.

The dance business did not seem to be profitable, so they closed the house, and Messrs. Lear and Vanderbilt, who had the leasing of it, very kindly allowed me to make the change. It is much more comfortable than the old log house.

"Mrs. Dickinson has just sent her little girls down to me to write you her kind regards.

"I must describe to you how the natives observed Christmas. Between twelve and one o'clock Christmas morning I was awakened by hearing persons coming up to my house. I arose, and from my window saw about sixty of my Indians standing in a double row in front of my house, with their lanterns and umbrellas, for it was raining heavily. Just as I looked out they commenced singing, ' While shepherds watched their flocks by night.' They sung that and another hymn, and then went quietly away. It seemed to me that nothing ever aroused my gratitude as that did. I did not know that there was anything more to come. But about nine o'clock in the morning I saw a large procession filing into my yard. First came the son of one of our prominent men, a boy about thirteen, carrying a large British flag. Perhaps some Sabbath-school class of boys would be willing to present our mission with an American flag, the Stars and Stripes. Next came the Christian chief, Toy-a-att. Then came all the leading men; then their wives, then my school. They walked in single file. I stood in my door, and as they walked past each one shook hands with me and wished me 'A Merry Christmas.' The old chief took my hand and said, 'A Merry Christmas,' and

A SALUTATION.

'God bless you, dear teacher,' and, much to my surprise, leaned forward and kissed me on the cheek. He had evidently learned his speech for the occasion, as he does not speak English. I wish I could describe their costumes. But as I have not time I will only say that the boy who carried the flag was dressed in light blue cashmere, covered over with gilt stars. He had also on a head-dress made of flowers and stars. There were about two hundred in the procession.

"During the holidays the natives got into many troubles, through the great quantities of whiskey that have been made here. It became so bad that Mr. Dennis gathered a *posse* of men last Thursday and made a raid on suspected parties. Eight distilleries were found and broken up. There have been eighteen in all destroyed. Yours truly,

"A. R. McFarland."

ALASKA FOX.

CHAPTER VI.

Indian Constitutional Convention—Great Speech of Toy-a att—Native Police—Indians making a Treaty of Peace—Need of a Home for Girls—Witchcraft—Home Commenced—Arrival of Rev. S. Hall Young.

> "Oh ! for God and native land,
> And his Word make strong your hand.
> Task—an angel might desire ;
> Task—your Christian zeal must fire !
> This your task, oh, seeing one,
> May it win, at last, ' Well done.' "

THE mission commenced the year 1878 with an important movement toward law. There were five hundred whites and a thousand Indians congregated in the place. Gambling, drunkenness and debauchery were rife.

The military had been withdrawn, and there were no officers or courts for the protection of life and redress of grievances.

In this condition of affairs a few chiefs and Indians who had renounced heathenism and gathered around the mission, feeling the need of some government, appointed Toy-a-att, Moses and Matthew as a police force to keep order and punish the guilty.

For a time it worked smoothly, but after a while Shus-taks, the leading heathen chief, rebelled, and

CONSTITUTIONAL CONVENTION. 167

told the Indians that the policemen had no authority. Consequently, to secure the sanction of popular opinion, a constitutional convention was called for February 3d, 1878. This convention lasted for two days, Mrs. A. R. McFarland being elected the presiding officer.

She thus writes concerning the convention :

"The school-house was packed full. We had a great many long speeches, until it began to grow dark. I had written out some laws, with which they seemed to be much pleased. But as it was now five o'clock in the afternoon, I proposed that they should adjourn until the next morning, and that I would take the rules home and copy them off ready for their signatures. The next morning at daybreak Shus-taks came out on the end of the Point, as he always does when he has anything to say to the people. He then made a great speech, telling them that he knew all about what he had been doing the day before, and that I was trying to make war between him and the other people.

"When we met at the school-house that morning we concluded to send an invitation to Shus-taks to come over and hear the laws read, and, if possible, conciliate him. He came, bringing five of his men with him. We also invited Mr. Dennis, the Deputy Collector of Customs, to be present.

"I had the first talk with Shus-taks. He was very hostile, and made bitter remarks. I tried to convince him that I had come up there to do him and his people good, and then read him the laws we had adopted.

"He replied that he would like to know what I had to do with the laws—that I had been sent there to teach school, and nothing more. He said that if Mr. Dennis and I went on, as we were now doing, that we would upset the town and bring war, and all the people would be killed. He said he supposed that I thought I was safe, but he would advise me to send for the soldiers to come back.

"Mr. Dennis then had a talk with him; but I do not think it made the least impression.

"Then Toy-a-att made a talk to Shus-taks—indeed preached him a solemn sermon. He told him that he was now an old man and could not live long; that he wanted him to give his heart to the Saviour, who had died for him; that if he did not, but died as he was living, he must be forever lost.

"Shus-taks replied that he did not care if he did go to hell-fire—that his people were all there. He then left the meeting.

"After he had gone the people all signed their names (or rather I wrote their names and they made their mark) to the following rules:

1st.

We concur in the action of Mr. I. C. Dennis, Deputy Collector of U. S. Customs, appointing Toy-a-att, Moses, Matthew, and Sam, to search all canoes and stop the traffic of liquor among the Indians.

2d.

We, who profess to be Christians, promise with God's help to strive as much as possible to live at peace with each other—to have no fighting, no quarrelling, no tale-bearing among us. These things are all sinful, and should not exist among Christians.

LAWS ENACTED

3d.

Any troubles that arise among the brethren, between husbands and wives, or any man leaves his wife, these brethren, Toy-a-att, Moses, Matthew, Aaron, and Lot, have authority to settle the troubles and decide what the punishment shall be ; and if fines are imposed, how much the fines shall be.

4th.

The authority of these brethren is binding upon all. And no person is to resist or interfere with them, as they are appointed by Mr. Dennis and Mrs. McFarland.

5th.

To all the above we subscribe our names.

The great speech of the convention was that of Chief Toy-a-att before a crowded audience of whites and Indians. We give it as reported in the Port Townsend *Weekly Argus :*

" My brothers and friends, I come before you to-day to talk a little, and I hope you will listen to what I say, and not laugh at me because I am an Indian. I am getting old, and have not yet many summers to live on this earth. I want to speak a little of the past history of us Stickeen Indians and of our present wants. In ages past, before white men came among us, the Indians of Alaska were barbarous, with brutish instincts.

" Tribal wars were continual, bloodshed and murder of daily occurrence, and superstition controlled our whole movements and our hearts.

" The white man's God we knew not of. Nature evinced to us that there was a first great cause ; beyond all that was blank. Our god was created by us ; that is, we selected animals and birds, the images of which we revered as gods.

"Natural instincts taught us to supply our wants from that which we beheld around us. If we wanted food, the waters gave us fish ; and if we wanted raiment, the wild animals of the woods gave us skins, which we converted to use. Implements of warfare and tools to work with we constructed rudely from stone and wood. [Here the speaker showed specimens of stone axes and weapons of warfare.]

"These," said he, holding them up to view, "we used in the place of the saws, axes, hammers, guns, and knives of the present time. Fire we discovered by friction. [Here he demonstrated how they produced fire.]

"In the course of time a change came over the spirit of our dreams. We became aware of the fact that we were not the only beings in the shape of man that inhabited this earth. White men appeared before us on the surface of the great waters in large ships, which we called canoes. Where they came from we knew not, but supposed that they dropped from the clouds. The ships' sails we took for wings, and concluded that, like the birds of the air, they could fly as well as swim. As time advanced, the white men who visited our country introduced among us everything that is produced by nature and the arts of man. They also told us of a God, a superior being, who created all things, even us, the Indians. They told us that this God was in the heavens above, and that all mankind were his children. These things were told us, but we could not understand them.

"At the present time we are not the same people that we were a hundred years ago. Contact and association with the white man has created a change in our habits and customs. We have seen and heard of the wonderful works of the white man. His ingenuity and skill has produced steamships, railroads, telegraphs, and thousands of other things. His mind is far-reaching ; whatever he desires he produces. His wonderful sciences enable him to understand nature and her laws. Whatever she produces he improves upon and makes useful.

"Each day the white man becomes more perfect in the arts and sciences, while the Indian is at a standstill. Why is this ? Is it because the God you have told us of is a white God, and that you, being of his color, have been favored by him?

"Why, brothers, look at our skin ; we are dark, we are not of your color, hence you call us Indians. Is this the reason that we are ignorant ; is this the cause of our not knowing our Creator?

"My brothers, a change is coming. We have seen and heard of the wonderful things of this world, and we desire to understand what we see and what we hear. We desire light. We want our eyes to become open. We have been in the dark too long, and we appeal to you, my brothers, to help us.

"But how can this be done? Listen to me. Although I have been a bad Indian, I can see the right road, and I desire to follow it. I have changed for the better. I have done away with all Indian superstitious habits. I am in my old age becoming civilized. I have learned to know Jesus, and I desire to know more of him. I desire education, in order that I may be able to read the Holy Bible.

"Look at Fort Simpson and at Metlakatla, British Columbia. See the Indians there. In years gone by they were the worst Indians on this coast, the most brutal, barbarous, and blood-thirsty. They were our sworn enemies, and were continually at war with us. How are they now? Instead of our enemies they are our friends. They have become partially educated and civilized. They can understand what they see and what they hear; they can read and write, and are learning to become Christians. These Indians, my brothers, at the places just spoken of, are British Indians, and it must have been the wish of the British Queen that her Indians should be educated. We have been told that the British Government is a powerful one, and we have also been told that the American Government is a more powerful one. We have been told that the President of the United States has control over all the people, both whites and Indians. We have been told how he came to be our great chief. He purchased this country from Russia, and in purchasing it he purchased us. We had no choice or say in change of masters. The change has been made, and we are content. All we ask is justice.

"We ask of our father at Washington that we be recognized as a people, inasmuch as he recognizes all other Indians in other portions of the United States.

"We ask that we be civilized, Christianized, and educated. Give us a chance, and we will show to the world that we can become peaceable citizens and good Christians. An effort has already been made by Christian friends to better our condition, and may God bless them in their work. A school has been established here, which, notwithstanding strong opposition by bad white men and by Indians, has done a good and great work among us.

"This is not sufficient. We want our chief at Washington to help us. We want him to use his influence toward having us a church built and in having a good man sent to us who will teach us to read the Bible and learn all about Jesus. And now, my brothers, to you I appeal. Help us in our efforts to do right. If you don't want to come to our church, don't laugh and make fun of us because we sing and pray.

"Many of you have Indian women living with you. I ask you to send them to school and church, where they will learn to become good women. Don't, my brothers, let them go to the dance-houses, for there they will learn to be bad and learn to drink whiskey.

"Now that I see you are getting tired of listening to me, I will finish by asking you again to help us in trying to do right. If one of us should be led astray from the right path, point out to us our error and assist us in trying to reform. If you will all assist us in doing good, and quit selling whiskey we will soon make Fort Wrangell a quiet place, and the Stickeen Indians will become a happy people. I now thank you all for your kind attention. Good-by."

ARRIVAL OF REV. JOHN G. BRADY.

"FORT WRANGELL, ALASKA, March 16th, 1878.
"DR. JACKSON.

"DEAR BROTHER : There has been a great time among the natives here this week. It seems that the Tongas and Stickeens have been enemies for a number of years ; but this winter they have become friends. This week the Tongas came to visit the Stickeens and have a grand ' Hee-Hee.' We all went down to the beach to see the Tongas come in. They had nine large canoes lashed together abreast. They were all dressed in their gayest colors, and made quite an imposing appearance. After landing they and the Stickeens had a sham battle, followed by a grand dance on the beach. They were all painted, and dressed in their native costumes. There were some 1500 of them present, besides all the whites in the settlement. It was a strange scene, and one long to be remembered. The dancing has been kept up all the week, day and night, and I suppose will be for some time to come.

"The great importance of our work here was more than ever felt, as I looked upon this multitude of immortal souls who had never heard of a crucified Saviour. And my earnest prayer was that with the coming of Rev. Mr. Brady, these people, who have never heard the Gospel, might have their eyes opened to the truth.

."Rev. Mr. Brady arrived by steamer on the 15th. It is a great encouragement to have him here. He went on to Sitka, but will return with the steamer.

"Two weeks ago Rev, Bishop Bompas (Episcopalian) came up on the Otter, but returned on the same boat.

"He reported that he had come to look up mission stations, but had no desire to come in where other churches were already on the ground. He spent a day in my school, and spoke to some of our citizens, highly commending the management and success of the school. I told him of my great desire to establish a home for young girls, and also how my heart had ached at the utter destitution of all comfort among those that were sick.

"He seemed to think that there should be a fund for the relief of the worthy suffering, and as for the 'Home,' he was sure if Christians in the East could be made to see the importance of it, that I would soon have all the money needed to build and furnish the necessary quarters.

"Before leaving he gave me $2, one for the 'Home' and the other to relieve sick Indians. He said he was poor, but wished to do something, and advised me to write East that the fund was commenced, and that every dollar that was added to it would help on the great and glorious work. I wish so much that some one else could take the school and I be allowed to give my entire time to the women and girls. If we had only some rooms for a home I am sure that some Ladies' Society would support it. The need is a most urgent one.

"Yours truly,

"A. R. McFARLAND."

"FORT WRANGELL, ALASKA, March 26th, 1878.

"DEAR BROTHER: On Sabbath morning Rev. Mr. Brady married, in the church, Toy-a-att (our Christian chief) and his wife, and Moses and his wife. The service was performed with the ring and all.

"On Monday some Indians came to my schoolroom and asked us to go to 'Shakes' and have a funeral service for a young man that had died the night before. Upon receiving the word Mr. Brady came up, the school was dismissed, and taking some of our people with us we went over to the house. They received us very kindly, and we had an interesting meeting. The heathen portion of the audience seemed to be very much impressed. They had intended to burn the body, according to the customs of their fathers. But before we came away the most prominent man among them made a speech, saying that he was 'going to have a hole made and bury the dead man as white men did.' He said if a minister came to live at Fort Wrangell, the missionary was to be the head, and they were bound to do whatever he told them. The hearts of these heathens seemed to be opened in a most wonderful manner. Everything seems to be ready for a great work to be done for Christ among this people, if we only had a minister here to carry it on. Mr. Brady goes by the steamer to Sitka.

"About two o'clock yesterday a messenger came with an invitation for Mr. Brady and myself to a wedding feast that Toy-a-att and Moses were giving in Matthew's house Of course we accepted the invitation. We were agreeably surprised to see how nicely

KING GEORGE'S PEOPLE. 177

they had everything arranged. Their tables were neatly set with clean white cloth. Two long tables extended clear across the house. You remember that Matthew's house has a raised platform extending around the wall of the building and three feet above the main ground floor. Upon this platform they had set a small table for Mr. Brady and myself. The dinner was good. They had crackers, butter, salmon, apricots, pies of different kinds, plum-pudding, tea, coffee, condensed milk, and white sugar. I have eaten plum-puddings made by white people that were not near as good as theirs. They had prepared great quantities of everything. The two long tables were filled three times, and every one had all they could eat. It was surprising to see how orderly and quietly everything was carried on in such a crowd.

"There were several of the Tongas and Hydah chiefs present. Mr. Brady had a long talk with them. A very fine and intelligent looking Tongas chief, who did most of the talking, asked when his people were to have schools and preachers. Mr. Brady replied by asking if nothing had been done for them. We were much surprised at his reply. He said that an English missionary had been there and offered to do something for them, but that they belonged to the United States, and did not want King George's people coming over to teach them ; that they would wait and look to American people for help. Mr. Brady assured them that they should have teachers as soon as they could be secured. This talk was had while the second and third tables were being served.

"After all had eaten, and the tables were carried out, Toy-a-att proposed that they should have a regular Indian dance, to show us how they did before they knew about God. They then dressed up in their Indian costumes, masked their faces, then came out and danced four different kinds of dances. After the dance they played a game called the flag-game. They drew us both into this game, which amused them very much. At the close Toy-a-att made a speech, saying that this was their last dance, that they had learned a better way, and did not intend to dance any more. He then turned around and presented us each with one of their musical instruments, saying they would now have no further use for them. The party then broke up, and all went home before dark. Yours truly,
"A. R. McFarland."

"Fort Wrangell, Alaska, June, 1878.

"Dear Brother : Shaaks (the head chief of these people) came home sick with a hemorrhage of the lungs, and died in four days. They kept the body lying in state (or rather sitting) until Sabbath. On Saturday they sent for me to decide whether they should burn or bury the body. Of course I decided that it was better to bury it. They said then it should be buried. On Sabbath they sent for me to take charge of the funeral, saying "they wanted me to come and pray like white people." So I took some of our Christian Indians and went and had religious service. They seemed very much pleased. None of Shaaks' people have ever attended church.

SHAAKS LYING IN STATE.

DISAPPOINTMENTS.

On Saturday evening I talked with the new chief, Shaak's brother. He promised me that he would attend church. Said he wanted to learn about God. Mr. Davidson secured a very good photograph of the dead chief as he was sitting in state, with all his Indian fixtures around him. Since Rev. Mr. Brady went to Sitka we have been doing the best we can, but it is hard work carrying on the Sabbath services.

"June 7.—Mr. Brady and Miss Kellogg write very encouragingly of the work at Sitka.

"My school is now averaging thirty-five scholars, which is very good for this season of the year. Many have gone to the mines and other places for work.

"Shus-taks has been pretty quiet since the revenue cutter came. He tried to make trouble about the time that Shaaks died, by reporting that Shaaks had been poisoned by some white person. I believe that Shus-taks will come around all right yet.

"June 13.—The steamer California came in last night, and we were again disappointed in the non-arrival of the minister. The delay in securing a minister makes me almost sick. The Indians, too, feel it very much. Toy-a-att and Lot came to me last night to know 'How many moons now till preacher comes?' I told them that I could not tell anything about it. I hoped he would come next steamer, but I could not tell. Toy-a-att laid his hand on his heart and said, '*Nica sick. Tum-tum. Wake-siah. Conaway Indian mama Louse. Nika sick, Tum-tum.*' (I have sad heart. By and by Indian all dead. I have sad, sad heart.) He felt so badly that he shed tears over it. I fear all this delay is going to cause the Indians to lose confidence in the church.

"July 8.—By the last steamer we heard that the minister was on board on his way here, so I had the girls clean up a house and get it all ready for him. This time we felt so sure that he would come that I had the men and boys bring in evergreens and trim up the school-room beautifully, but when the steamer came, and no minister, the disappointment was correspondingly great. The Indians said, 'Well, we will not do anything more. It is no use. We do not believe any person is coming at all.' I cannot blame them. I have not been so depressed since coming here. The work is greatly suffering and the success of the mission greatly imperilled by the long delay in the arrival of a minister.

"Then the idea has been held out that we were going to build a church this season, and yet there is no one here to take the lead, and consequently nothing has been done.

"Then, to add to all the other discouragements, a Catholic priest came up on this steamer. No person knows what he is going to do. But the indications are that he has come to stay. I would not be surprised to see him at once commence the erection of a church. If he expects to do anything here, he will be shrewd enough to take advantage of the disappointment of the Indians at the long delay in the coming of a minister.

"The captain of the steamer has kindly invited me to accompany his wife and daughter on a free trip to Sitka, which I have accepted.

KLAWOCK—APPEAL FOR SCHOOL. 183

"SITKA, July 10.—I find Miss Kellogg very happy and much interested in her work.

"Rev. Mr. Brady has just returned from a missionary tour to the Hoonas Indians, and will make application for a missionary for them. There is also a new settlement of Americans up here, where we should have a missionary at once. Oh, how long will the church sleep and let these people perish? Can nothing be done to secure more help?

"July 10.—We have been lying all day in the steamer at the new settlement of Klawock.

"The principal white men have visited me, to learn what was necessary for them to do to secure a missionary. The Indians also have been to see me. They ask, 'Why can't we have a school as well as the Indians at Sitka or Fort Wrangell?' One of the Americans says he is confident we could have a school of one hundred Indians here. There are also a number of white children, and very great need of a mission. It is a dirty, muddy, disagreeable village, much more so than Wrangell, and nothing but the love of the work and love to the Saviour would induce missionaries to live at such a place. And yet it ought to be occupied.

"There is a saw-mill here. Lumber is cheap, and the people will do all they can to assist the mission. Surely it is a call from God. Will the Church enable the board to respond?

"I have had two schools in operation since spring. Up the beach were a lot of wild natives that I could not induce to come into our school. I felt so distressed about them that I concluded that if they were too shy to come to me I would go to them. I rented an old log building on the point in their neighborhood and opened school. I have from forty-five to sixty in attendance. I teach them from the blackboard. This school meets in the afternoon. After I had gone a few times they asked me if I would not come Sunday and have church for them. Consequently I hold a little service with them on the Sabbath afternoons. They seem much interested. By and by 1 hope they may be induced to attend the other church and school.

"We have had more witchcraft here, and the effect has been very bad on the minds of the young people. Some of my brightest and best scholars have been led away by it. As we have no kind of law, none of the whites felt that they had any right to interfere. It has frequently been said to me, 'If you will get a minister here, so that the Indians will see that he is permanent, and one who will make them understand he is determined to break up all such things, it will more than anything else tend to prevent the recurrence of such scenes.'

"Yours truly, A. R. McFARLAND."

"FORT WRANGELL, ALASKA, Sept. 3d, 1878.

"DEAR BROTHER : Rev. Mr. Young has been very busy since his arrival last month. He has made a very favorable impression both on the whites and the natives. We all like him very much. Last Sabbath he was called upon to attend the funeral of an old woman who died on Saturday. When we went to the house we were shocked to see the dead body of another woman wrapped in a blanket and lying on the floor. We were still more shocked to find that she had hung herself but a short time before. It was the effect of witchcraft.

"I have not yet moved into the hospital building, as I have nothing to begin with. I am exceedingly anxious to get the 'Home' started. There are six young girls whom I ought to take right away, as the miners are coming into town for the winter. I tremble for these poor children lest it should be too late to save them. I have turned the responsibility of the school over to Mr. Young, and feel as if a great load had been taken off my shoulders. He preaches to the whites at three o'clock every Sabbath afternoon. They come out very well, and seem to be greatly interested.

"Sept. 11, 1878.—The steamer has just come in, and how rejoiced I am to hear that the Board of Home Missions has commissioned Miss Dunbar. I wish she was here now to take charge of the fall school. I also received a very kind letter from Dr. Cyrus Dickson, with the renewal of my commission for another year.

"I realize more and more the difficulties I will have to contend with in opening this 'Home,' but I also feel the necessity laid upon me of going forward. There are several girls here now who will be lost if I do not take them at once. Of course there are a great many more, but these I feel particularly interested in, because they have been in school and have made considerable progress. Being pretty and smart, they are just the ones the white men will try to get possession of. I have written many letters and made appeals in many directions, but so far have received little encouragement to go on, and yet I feel that I must do it. Mr. Young has been urging me to get moved and make a beginning. He feels the necessity of it. I will try to move this month into the old hospital building, but of course we will have nothing to begin with in the way of furniture. Still I have faith to believe that it will come in due time.

"Mrs. Dickinson has just been in with a woman who is the mother of one of my scholars, a pretty girl of thirteen. She was about to start up the river with the child to make money to buy 'muck-a-muck' for the winter. The woman is determined to go herself, but after much persuasion consented to leave the girl with me. So you see the 'Home' is started.

"October 17.— . . . My girls are contented and happy. Lest some should think that I acted unwisely in taking them before their support was pledged, permit me to say that I could not do otherwise. I dared not delay even for a week.

"Of course I feel much anxiety about the means to carry on the work. I know it will be a great struggle for a while, but my trust is in the prayer-hearing God, whose work it is. I hope to hear by the next steamer that some societies have assumed the support of these girls.

"Mr. Young is very busy securing what funds he can here toward the erection of a church.

"Mr. J. M. Vanderbilt, to whom we have been indebted for many facilities, has paid the rent for us

THE HOSPITAL—A SQUARE-ROOFED TWO-STORY BUILDING USED FOR THE MCFARLAND INDUSTRIAL HOME FROM SEPTEMBER 1878 TO 1880.

ARRIVAL OF REV. S. HALL YOUNG. 189

on the hospital building for one year, as a contribution from his wife. Truly yours,
"A. R. McFARLAND."

In August, 1878, the Rev. S. Hall Young, of Parkersburg, West Virginia, who had been commissioned by the Board of Home Missions the previous spring, reached Fort Wrangell.

Graduating with high honors at Allegheny Theological Seminary, he entered upon his work with great zeal and earnestness, and was very gladly welcomed by Mrs. McFarland. At the very outset of his work Mr. Young was confronted with demonstrations of witchcraft. Consequently he held a convention of the people to put it down. This convention lasted five days. Mrs. McFarland writes :

"FORT WRANGELL, ALASKA, Nov. 9th, 1878.

"DEAR BROTHER : The witchcraft excitement has again broken out and given Mr. Young much trouble. He has shown great wisdom and courage in quelling it without the loss of life. Kootlan, the oldest of the Stickeen chiefs, died this week after a long illness. Although he belonged to the heathen Indians, yet they sent for Mr. Young to attend the funeral. Shustaks lost his wife this week, and is making great preparations to burn the body next Sabbath. Mr. Young and I both visited her during her illness. Her friends firmly believe that she was bewitched.

"The more fully we become acquainted with Mr. Young, the more we are impressed that the Lord has sent us just the right man. He makes a splendid missionary.

"I am very much pleased with the proposition to ask a Christmas offering for my Home. We are living on faith now.

"December 5th, 1878.

"Mr. Young has recently held a five days' council with the chiefs and principal men of the Stickeen nation. The different bands of the nation were not good friends. Each of the chiefs had his following, and they would not attend church together. Since the council many more have been attending church. If the council result in breaking down their jealousies, an important point will have been gained. Mr. Young has also taken hold of the witchcraft operations with great vigor, and, I think, will be able to break them up.

"Our school is doing nicely. We greatly need another teacher.

"The council has opened up the way for much more visiting among the people. But with the school and Home on my hands it is impossible for me to do more. Yours truly,

"A. R. McFarland."

Rev. Mr. Young writes:

"Fort Wrangell, Alaska, Dec. 5, 1878.

"Dear Dr. Jackson: We have gained a victory over witchcraft. Shus-taks and his wife were both sick, and of course they must blame some one with having worked 'bad medicine' against them. Young Shaaks, successor of the head chief and nephew to Shus-taks, gathered up his friends and caught an old man, one of our church attendants, and accused

REV. S. HALL YOUNG.

him of being 'bad medicine.' They carried him to Shus-tak's house, stripped him naked, tied him most cruelly hand, foot, and head, and put him into a dark hole under the floor. This happened at night. The next morning the clerk of the Custom-House and myself went over to the house where all Shus-taks and Shaaks' friends were assembled. They were very determined to resist any encroachment on their ancient customs, but we were equally firm and persistent that they should release him, and tie up nobody else without first consulting us. This they at length did. Although angry at first, they soon saw the reasonableness of our request. Shaaks has promised to come to church and bring all his followers. Mrs. Shus-taks has since died, and, contrary to the wish of all his friends, her husband had her burned. Shaaks is rather a fine young man, and professes to have renounced his belief in witchcraft.

"I have been canvassing for the church and school. I expect to raise about $600, mostly from the Indians, to build a neat church, with seating capacity for two hundred and fifty. Will cost about $2500. We can get undressed lumber here for $22 per 1000, and dressed at $31. We will need a large school-house, as the native population is large and increasing monthly. All the educational influences for this whole region will centre here. Six tribes look to us for light. Next season I expect a school of three hundred pupils. Our hope is in the young. They learn rapidly, and are delighted with the school. We have selected a good location on the first bluff above the beach, containing two acres. It was presented by

Mr. Lear. We will commence work clearing off the brush and draining it at once. We shall proceed only as we have the funds, therefore we hope the friends of the mission will be prompt with their contributions.

"I have not yet figured on the cost of a Home for Girls. It depends entirely on the number of girls the Ladies' Societies will support. You see the needs of the work have no limit, save the probability of support.

"We could in a year or two gather into the Home a large number of interesting girls who will otherwise be lost. I do hope that this enterprise of all the institutions upon this coast will receive the support of the Christian world. It is essential to the enlightenment of the people. Unless these girls are sheltered and saved, our preaching will largely be in vain. *Mrs. McFarland has acted wisely in founding this protectorate. It was absolutely necessary.* We were compelled by the urgency of the cases of several girls to open it before their support was guaranteed. We could not help it. And now we trust the Presbyterian Church will not let it fail for want of funds. We have received many encouraging promises, but are now in pressing need of the money. Oh, if some Christian would endow this institution, what a noble work he would do for this people!

"Mrs. McFarland is exactly fitted to be the matron of such a home. The women of the place love her as a mother. She has been offered large salaries and easy positions elsewhere, but remains here, spending her time, great energies, and private funds to help

CATECHETICAL CLASS ORGANIZED. 195

this work. She has had a severe struggle to get started, but I hope her heaviest trials are past. She merits the fullest confidence and most generous support of the Church. I am most happy in having such a helper.

"We were much disappointed in not securing another teacher by last steamer. The pressure of work is beyond the strength of Mrs. McFarland and myself. The Indians come to me more and more for counsel on all manner of questions. I never dreamed of having such a weight of care.

"I am about organizing a catechetical class, to train material for elders, deacons, and members. I preach twice each Sabbath to the natives and once to the whites. Our congregations are large and orderly. Sabbath-school is immediately after morning service. I hope you will be able to stir up a great interest in this field. The next few years will practically decide the fate of many tribes on this coast. I thank you for what you have done and are doing for these poor people. God bless you.

"Your brother in Christ,
"S. HALL YOUNG."

A PUFFIN.

CHAPTER VII.

Sketch of Sitka—Arrival of Rev. John G. Brady and Miss Fannie
E. Kellogg—Commencement of School—Missionary Journeys
of Mr. Brady—Marriage of Miss Kellogg—School of Mr. Alonzo
E. Austin.

' The snowy peaks that north and south now rise to summits grand,
Stood here the ocean's tide beside, and watched it near at hand.
The spirit of the storms kept one, and when his robe he shook,
The roar that swept the clouds along was heard to far Chinook ;
'Twas there the spirit dwelt whose fires flash from the mountain's
    shroud
In lightning strokes that signal when shall peal the stormy
    cloud—
Dread spirits, born of gloomy power, whose anger sometimes
    woke
In jealous wrath, and then would flash the lightning's fiery
    stroke ;
Then thunder with its muffled roll would answer peal on peal,
And fires would light the mountain-side like blows of flint on
    steel."

SITKA, Alaska, has had a varied history. The head-quarters of Russian supremacy in the North Pacific, it was once a proud commercial city, the centre of an extensive commerce, and capital of a large province, with many schools and seminaries. Here Baron Romanoff for years ruled as governor with despotic hand. The castle, once the abode of Russia's proud nobles, still crowns the hill. The officers' quarters, barracks, and club-house still remain. The church, built in the form of a Greek

REAR VIEW OF GREEK CHURCH, SITKA.

cross, with its emerald green dome and roof, its chime of bells, its queer interior arrangement, its paintings, rich vestments, and candlesticks and chandeliers of massive silver—all speak of Russian power. The old stockade, from whose loop-holes upon occasion during the Romanoff dominion poured the death-dealing ball and shot, is now partly in ruins.

Sitka has a beautiful island-studded bay, said to equal in picturesqueness the Bay of Naples or Rio Janeiro. Mount Edgecumbe, an extinct volcano, discovered by Bodega in 1775, still guards the entrance to the bay, while the sharp, snowy summit of Vostovia, surrounded by a group of peaks and glaciers, stands guard in the rear. The opening gold mines and the great salmon-canning interests seem now to hold out a prospect of future prosperity.

The bay was first visited by Baranoff in 1799, who built a fort which he called Fort Archangel Gabriel, and took possession of the country for Russia. Three years later the Indians rose, captured the fort, and murdered all the officers and thirty men. In 1804 Baranoff returned and recaptured the town and built Fort Archangel Michael, the settlement taking the name of New Archangel. From 1809 shipbuilding became one of the active industries of the place. In 1810 the place was visited by the Enterprise, one of the ships of John Jacob Astor's fur company. The same year a Greek priest arrived in a sloop-of-war, to minister unto the colonists. The first resident physician did not reach Sitka until ten years later.

The growth and importance of the place were finally assured in 1832, when Baron Wrangell transferred the capital of Russian America from St. Paul to Sitka. In 1834 it was made the seat of a bishopric,

THE BAY OF SITKA, ALASKA.

SCHOOLS. 201

and Father Veniaminoff made bishop. This eminent prelate was afterward recalled to Russia and made the head of the Greek Church. 'In 1837 the first steam-engine was introduced into the colony. It came from Boston with a cargo of whiskey and rum.

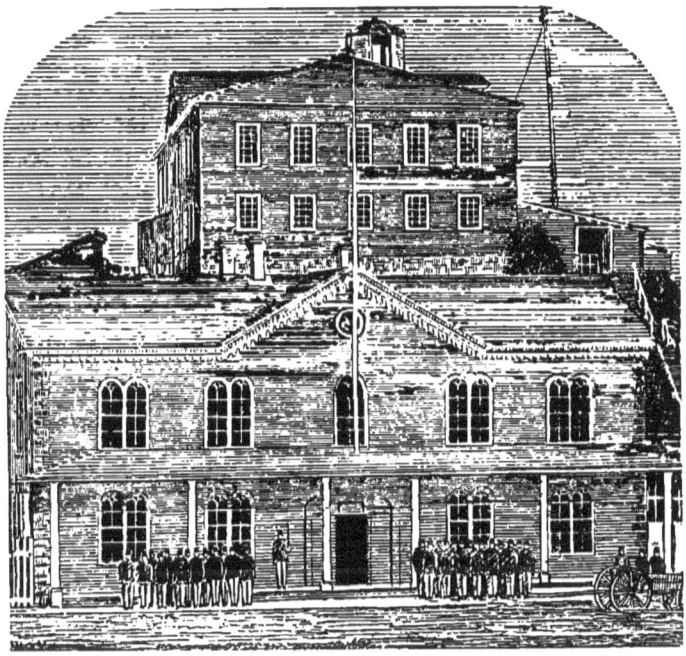

THE CASTLE AND CUSTOM-HOUSE, SITKA.

About the same time a school was established for the children of the employés of the Russian Fur Company. In 1839 it fell into the hands of Etolin, who greatly increased its usefulness.

In 1841 an ecclesiastical school of the Greek Church was established at Sitka, which in 1845 was raised to the rank of a seminary. In this school were taught arithmetic, geography, history, book-keeping, navigation, geometry and trigonometry, and the Russian and English languages. In 1845 the first school was established for the natives. These schools were discontinued at the time of the American occupation in 1867, and no other supplied their place until the arrival of Rev. John G. Brady and Miss Kellogg, Presbyterian missionaries, in 1878.

Of his work there Rev. Mr. Brady writes:

"SITKA, ALASKA, May, 1878.

"REV. SHELDON JACKSON, D.D.

"DEAR DOCTOR: We arrived here the night of April the 11th. Our first meeting occurred on Sunday in the castle. The day was charming, for the clouds had vanished, the sun was warm, and the scenery was all that could be asked. Far out beyond the harbor, protected by innumerable green islets, lay the vast Pacific, in a sort of rolling calmness. At another point rose the funnel-topped Edgecumbe, crested with snow. Back of the town, and as far down the coast as the eye can reach, we have all the variety of grand mountain scenery. When these days come all nature seems to be still with solemnity, and one appears to be near the presence-chamber of the Almighty. Alaska scenery has a peculiar effect upon my emotions.

"The castle has been stripped of everything, and is in a dilapidated condition. As we began to sing some of the Moody and Sankey hymns, the Indians began to steal in and squat themselves on the floor

REV. JOHN G. BRADY.

along the wall. Most of them had their faces painted black ; some were black and red, and a few had the whole face black with the exception of the right eye, which was surrounded with a coat of red. All but a few of the chiefs were in their bare feet, and wrapped in blankets of various colors.

"Sitka Jack is the chief who seems to have the most influence among them, and he is their orator. He and Annahootz, the war chief, were clad in some old suits of the naval officers who have been here. They think a great deal of the buttons, shoulder-pieces and the like. Several wore soldiers' caps. The rest were bareheaded.

"The natives along the coast from Cape Fox to Mount St. Elias, speak the same tongue. Mr. Cohen, a Jew who keeps a store here, kindly volunteered to hunt up the old Russian interpreter. This man is about sixty years old. He is a half-breed. The Russian American Fur Company took him, when a boy, and educated him for a priest to the natives ; but for some reason he was never ordained to that office. He has always been employed as interpreter. He speaks both languages well, and can read and write the Russian. Mr. George Kastrometinoff turned my English into Russian, and the interpreter turned that into good Indian. The people listened very attentively to all that I had to say. Jack, becoming impatient to speak, broke into a gesticulating speech, telling how bad they were heretofore, fighting and killing one another. Now they were glad that they were going to have a school and a church, and people to teach them. After him Annahootz took the floor and made an emphatic speech, approving all that we had told them.

"I explained to them why we wished them to go to school, and the advantages which they would have if they would learn English. I centred everything upon the Bible, and tried to impress upon their minds its value to all men, because it is God speaking to us when we read it.

"Jack asked the people whether they liked what we had said, and after some talk among themselves they all said, ' Yes.' Mr. Francis and several miners were present. They expressed themselves as surprised to see the Indian consent so readily and act so heartily and with such straightforwardness.

"We held but one service that day, as it had lasted several hours. There were about one hundred and twenty-five persons present. This was rather a small number for Sitka, since there are over one thousand who live in the village. Many have gone off to trade and hunt ; they will return in two moons.

"I hired some Indians, and we all worked hard to put the upper floor of the soldiers' barracks in trim for our school and church services. Mr. Whitford, who bought nearly everything which the soldiers left, sold us twenty benches, a stove, cord of wood, two brooms, and a box of chalk. The Russian priest loaned us a blackboard with half-inch cracks between the boards. These things, together with two tables, make up the list of our furniture. The school opened on Wednesday, April 17th, with fifty present, and after asking God's blessing upon this beginning of a work, which will surely prove to be one of the most interesting in the history of missions, we began with A B C. It is a real pleasure to teach these people, for they are anxious to learn, and take right hold. They have bright intellects. The progress which they have made in the past month is a matter of amazement to me. There are thirteen now reading in the primer, and twenty-five have learned all the

THE BARRACKS, USED AS A SCHOOL-ROOM.

large letters. We have but six primers. This want of apparatus retards the work very much. Miss Kellogg has been careful to see that they do not learn in the parrot manner. They are taught the meaning of what they learn. They have learned 'Hold the Fort' and three or four more tunes, which they sing well. At some of our services over three hundred have been present.

"If our churches had known the facts concerning this people, and the wonderful coast upon which they live, missionaries would have been sent out years ago. The money spent in teaching and Christianizing these people will not be thrown away. 'Blessed are they which do hunger and thirst after righteousness : for they shall be filled.' This promise will surely be fulfilled to these people, for they are hungering and thirsting for more light. It would be a great wrong for the Church to neglect these people longer.

"I hope that before the leaves fall we shall be able to organize the Presbytery of Alaska. This will be a great thing for this Territory, which has been so wilfully misrepresented to the public. Such a body can be the source of information concerning the people and the country and its resources which will be trusted by the reading public.

"There has been no ice in Sitka this last winter, and very little snow fell. *The tops of the rain-barrels did not freeze to the thickness of a knife-blade.* Since I came here I have planted a large garden in peas, potatoes, lettuce, onions, turnips, and other vegetables. Most of these plants are now up. Nearly every vegetable that has been tried does well, beans and cucumbers excepted. Small fruits, such as strawberries, currants, gooseberries and the like, do very well and have a rich flavor. Cauliflower, cabbage, and celery do especially well. People are slow to believe such statements when they look at the map and find Sitka in 57° 3' north latitude.

"I came here expecting to find about the lowest

grade of people on the globe. In all my journey from New York to Sitka I received but very few words of encouragement from those who knew my mission. I now *know* that the people of our country are ignorant in regard to the people and resources of this grand system of archipelagoes. There are several miners here in Sitka who have been among the Indians since 1849, and are thoroughly informed in regard to customs, habits, mental powers, etc., of the various tribes in the gold regions. These men say that the Alaska Indians are in all respects superior to those on the plains. They build good, permanent houses. They store up supplies of food when fish, berries, and the like are in season. They will do hard work, and are always anxious to be employed. An officer of a steamboat which plies on the Stickeen told me that whenever he hired an Indian to chop so many cords of wood, and to have it at a certain place, he was sure to find the contract strictly fulfilled. The Cassiar miners in British Columbia employ them constantly in packing, chopping, and in doing all kinds of hard work. They are self-supporting.

"This part of Alaska abounds in food. Yesterday I bought four codfish for ten cents, and a string of black bass for five cents. A silver salmon, weighing thirty-eight to forty pounds, is sold for fifteen or twenty cents. Last week I bought fifteen dozen fresh clams for ten cents, and about twenty pounds of halibut for the same price. Ducks, geese, grouse, and snipe are abundant and cheap. A good ham of venison will bring fifty cents. In season berries are gathered by the bushel.

"These natives are very saving of anything to which the least value is attached. Some of the chiefs are worth six or eight thousand dollars in blankets, houses, skins, and the like. Some are wealthy on account of their slaves. The invention of these people is remarkable. Their canoes are perfect. Some of these are very large, holding three or four tons. They carve out all sorts of toys illustrating their mythology.

"Some of them devote their time to making jewelry, a thing of which they are all fond. Hydah John has done a great deal of work at Wrangell for the miners, in the way of rings, bracelets, and pins. One fellow here at Sitka labored for a long time in trying to make a watch! Nearly everything that they use has some sort of carving on it--their halibut-hooks, knife-handles, spoons, pipes, baskets, dancing apparatus, etc. This talent could be cultivated and made a source of income to them.

"Your brother in Christ,

"JOHN G. BRADY."

Miss Kellogg writes:

"SITKA, ALASKA, October, 1878.

"DEAR SIR: Our school has proved a success, and the advancement of the scholars has been a surprise to every one. For a time they were very irregular at the opening in the morning, but discovering that the larger scholars were very fond of writing (that they might be like Americans), I made it the first exercise after the opening service. Very few of them are tardy now. As far as possible, I give them object words for copy, requiring them to spell all out. I then pronounce it in English, and then give them the equivalent Indian word, that they may know what they are writing about. After writing a dozen lines, the English words are impressed upon their minds. They are stimulated to do well, as the one who takes the most pains gets a straight line or inventive drawing lessons.

"Two young men who have been only a few weeks in the school are in multiplication in arithmetic. They also have a perfect knowledge of notation, and can write or tell me the most difficult numbers.

"Each Friday evening we have a singing-school. Last week I told them that they could not be American men until they could whistle 'Yankee Doodle.' They caught the air at once. They are extremely fond of music, and have learned the air of many of Sankey's hymns. The hymn 'Come to Jesus' having much repetition, they have learned the English words.

"A week ago Sunday, the benches were all full, and the people seemed greatly interested. Forty-three remained at Sabbath-school. In four Sabbaths they committed the first two verses of the 23d Psalm, so that even those who could not say another word in English could repeat them perfectly.

"We have had a funeral and wedding. Captain Jack has had a rather bad reputation. He is, however, a good-natured Indian, and since the wedding ceremony calls himself a Christian. He has given up drinking, and has not tasted a drop for four months. He says, 'Me drink no more.' I have explained to him the temperance pledge, and as he can write his name he is anxious to sign one. I have tried to impress upon him the solemnity of the pledge, and that it would be a very sad thing if he broke it. I think at no distant day a little temperance society could be established here. Jack says that he wants to be good just as soon as he can learn how. Poor fellow, he needs the prayers of Christians.

"In consequence of his sobriety he was retained at a salmon-cannery until the last hand was discharged for the season. Returning with his wages, he bought some good clothing for church; also a nice calico dress and silk handkerchief and shawl for his wife. On the following Sabbath she had the handkerchief on her head. Meeting him afterward, I said, 'Jack, the next article you buy for Mary must be a hat, that she may look as well as the Fort Wrangell women, who have nice gloves, collars, neckties,' etc. Last Saturday they came to my house to show me his purchases—a muslin dress, which he wished me to show her how to make just like mine, two hats (a straw and velvet), a pair of gloves, and a green ribbon for a tie. I gave her collars and cuffs to complete the outfit. Jack is very proud of her, and in her new rig she is styled the 'belle of the city.'

"Mr. Brady succeeded in procuring the signatures of all the merchants to an agreement that they would send for no more molasses for rum, but the next steamer brought a large cargo of brown sugar. Even this is an improvement.

"Dick says, 'When molasses plenty, *hoochinoo* * (rum) two bits a bottle; plenty Indian buy rum. When rum two dollars a bottle, nobody buys.' The manufacture of rum must be stopped before these people can ever become Christianized.

"Truly yours,
"FANNIE E. KELLOGG."

"SITKA, ALASKA.

"DEAR DOCTOR: I have just returned from a missionary visit to the Hoonas. Indeed, I have recently made two canoe voyages, carrying with me provisions, blankets, and gun. The one was to the Hoonas, upon Chicagoff Island, and the other to the Kootsnoos and Litsuhquins, on Admiralty Island. Several times the canoe came near being lost in the chopping seas. The larger part of the time I was wet from the spray dashing over us. I preached boldly against witchcraft and the medicine-men, against gambling, drunkenness, and licentiousness. I took with me to the Hoonas a magic-lantern and some fine views of the Holy Land. You may imagine the astonishment of these people, who rarely ever see a white man. I exhibited on two nights. On the second night, Charlie, the interpreter, asked me to let

---

* Hoo-chi-noo, a rum distilled by the natives of Alaska from molasses. Their distillery is a very simple affair, being two discarded kerosene oil cans, and the long hollow root of the seaweed for a pipe. Hoo-chi-noo is the name of the tribe that first manufactured it. They were taught by a discharged soldier.

the views of Jesus raising Lazarus, Jairus' daughter, and Jesus walking on the water remain a longer time, as the people liked to see them. I had been talking to them about Jesus during the mornings. They are an interesting people, and something should be done for them.

"One day when we were among the icebergs which come down from one of the glaciers in Cross Sound, we came across one of the leading men. He was dressed in citizens' clothes, and had a good canoe and three strong men. We took him aboard. He showed some good testimonials which had been given him without solicitation. The next day he came and brought with him another leader and his son. This gave me an opportunity to speak to them, for Shukoff, my interpreter, was with me. They all knew what was going on in Sitka. After talking to them for some time they replied that they had been told that there was a God, and they believed that there was, but that they knew very little about him. They would be very happy to have some one come and teach them what is right and what God wants them to do. I asked if they would like to have their children go to school. They replied, 'Very much; but we are afraid that they can't learn well, like the children at Sitka. For they are close to white men, and hear them, but we do not know one word.' I assured them that the children would do well, for they would have less to draw them away from school. They said that their people wanted to become civilized, but they knew that some of the other tribes did not care to become so, but they thought that

MARRIAGE OF REV. S. HALL YOUNG. 215

their jealousy would be excited if they saw them doing well. They said that they would help build a school-house. Now here is a tribe ready for the Gospel, and the circumstances are all favorable, for they are sensible people, but little given to *hoochinoo* —far away from the whites, and are, therefore, virtuous. They have a home delightful for its scenery, and its shelter is close to some of the grandest sights on the globe, and they support themselves. If we could only anticipate the miners by three years, untold misery and vice would be prevented. The miners are coming, however, and are beginning to prospect, working in toward the sources of the Yukon. Your brother in Christ,

"JOHN G. BRADY."

In December, 1878, Miss Kellogg was married to Rev. S. Hall Young, of Fort Wrangell, and removed from Sitka to her new home. Upon her departure the school was suspended until the fall of 1879, when Mr. Alonzo E. Austin, of New York, at the invitation of the citizens, reopened it with sixty pupils.

In January, 1880, the Board of Home Missions appointed Rev. G. W. Lyons as missionary to Sitka, and Miss Olinda A. Austin, daughter of Mr. Alonzo E. Austin, as missionary teacher.

CHAPTER VIII.

Appeal for Funds for Mission Buildings—The Response—Joy at the Mission—Arrival of Dr. Corlies and Family—Coming of the Roman Catholics—Arrival of Miss Maggie J. Dunbar as Teacher —Visit of Rev. Henry Kendall, D.D., and others—Rejoicing of the Indians— Organization of the Church—Erection of Buildings.

" Pity the Red Man ! scattered and peeled,
Smitten and wounded, yet scorning to yield ;
Prairie and forest and lake we're his own,
Now he must wander, sad, homeless, and lone.

Hasten ! he stands on the farthermost shore ;
Haughty, intrepid, but loath to implore ;
Pilot his bark o'er the fathomless flood ;
Lead him to pardon. to Heaven, to God."

Rev. P. BEVAN.

THE prominent events in the history of Alaska missions for 1879 were the appeal for funds for the erection of mission buildings at Fort Wrangell, the erection of those buildings, the organization of the Fort Wrangell Presbyterian Church, and the visit of Rev. Henry Kendall, D.D., and party.

Dr. Kendall and myself, in addition to our missionary duties, were a commission of the United States Government, being officially requested by the Hon. John Sherman, Secretary of the United States Treasury (who has the supervision of Alaska affairs), to make him a report upon the condition of the native population, which we did upon our return. We also sent a report to the Hon. Carl Schurz, Secretary of the Interior, who replied with a letter of congratulations upon the success of the school at Fort Wrangell, and recommended an application to Congress for a grant for educational purposes in Alaska.

Mrs. McFarland felt, from the very commencement of the mission, the need of a "Home" into which she could gather such promising girls as were in danger of being sold, and train them up to be the future Christian teachers, wives, and mothers of their people.

Among a people where heathenism crushes out a mother's love and turns her heart to stone—where for a few blankets a mother will sell her own daughter for a week, a month, or for years—she found that her brightest and most promising pupils where those who were in the greatest danger. As they improved their advanages in the mission school, it manifested itself in their external appearance. They began to comb their hair more smoothly, to dress more neatly, and keep their persons more cleanly. Their dull, stolid countenances began to light up with intelligence. They became more attractive; and as their attractions increased, white men were the more anxious to buy them for base purposes.

Again and again Mrs. McFarland had to interpose to save her school-girls from lives of sin. One time she rescued one, a girl of not over eleven years, from a white man who had his arm around her on the street, and was trying to force and coax her to his house. At another time a white man went to the home of one of her pupils—an orphan girl—and holding out a handful of money rattled it before her eyes, saying that she could have all the money she wanted to buy nice clothes with if she would go and live with him. Upon another occasion one of her pupils came to her with tears, telling how her mother had sold her for fifteen or twenty blankets, and beseeching Mrs. McFarland to intercede with her mother, as she did not wish to live such a life.

Again and again her pupils, having been thus sold by their own mothers, have frantically clung to her, imploring her to save them.

During 1878 the pressure steadily increased month by month, and the necessity of such a Home more imperative.

Month after month she sent the most touching appeals to the Ladies' Societies for funds to commence the Home. Day after day, with a heart burdened for the daughters of this people, she went into her room, and with an agony that at times could not find expression in words, besought that God, who controls all hearts, would touch some, and raise up helpers. It was the cry of great need and sore distress.

Letters were received from various sections of the Church expressing a warm interest in the work, but no funds came.

While the church waited and the women of Alaska perished, the providence of God interposed, and the Home was commenced October 12th, 1878.

Katy, one of the school-girls, fourteen years of age, who had attended the school from the commencement, was about to be taken up the river and sold to the miners by her mother. Mrs. McFarland, hearing of it, took Mrs. Dickinson with her and started to visit the family, who lived over on the island. When they reached the point where they usually crossed, the tide was so high they could not get over. By signs they attracted Katy's attention, who came across in a canoe. She was sent back for her mother, who came over. There for an hour and a half, seated on a rock by the shore in a pouring rain, Mrs. McFarland pleaded with that heathen mother until she promised not to take Katy away. But the next week the mother broke her promise, and tried to compel her daughter to accompany her to the mines. The canoe was prepared, and the mother took her seat; the blankets, provisions, and younger children were in their places, but the little girl lingered on the shore. The mother ordered her in, threatening her with all manner of terrible things. The child hesitated, crying and begging most piteously. Finally, when they would have put her in by force, the little girl, straightening herself up, said, "Mother, you may kill me, but I will not go with you and live a life of sin."

She then ran into the woods and hid. When her mother had gone she came out and claimed Mrs. McFarland's protection.

Then a bright-eyed little girl of twelve years, who was about to be sold, having learned better things in the school, came begging Mrs. McFarland to save her, and thus a second was added to the Home.

Without furniture and without means, the enterprise began in the house kindly rented for the work by Mr. Vanderbilt. It is a large two-storied structure, well suited for the purpose. The Home being commenced, the necessity was upon the Church to provide for permanent buildings.

In this exigency, corresponding with Mrs. Julia McNair Wright, whose pen and talents are ever at the service of the Church, it was agreed that she and myself should write a series of appeals to the Church, to contribute, as a Christmas offering, the funds necessary for the erection of these buildings. This was done.

Mrs. Wright closed one of her articles with the following touching appeal :

"O mothers of our Church, every one of you who holds a baby girl on your knee, see in her face the pleading of that babe cast out in cold woods to die! In the name of Him who blessed the little children, give something, even if the veriest mite, to this Home. O you mothers of these dear young girls, every one whose home is made fairer by a daughter's face, give something to save these other girls from shame and anguish, something to help us teach these other mothers how great a boon a little maiden may be at her own fireside. The proposal is to make this Home for Alaskan girls the Christmas gift of our Presbyterian women to their Lord. Mothers, wives, sisters, daughters, friends, can you now prepare your Christmas gifts for your kindred and acquaintance, and send nothing, not one dollar, to this Christmas gift for our Lord ? Ah, better that there should be

SUCCESS OF THE APPEAL. 221

a little less, and not our choicest guest forgotten. Let us have a grand, warm-hearted response; let each, according to their ability, send to the Home Board a gift marked, 'For the Girls' Home in Alaska.'"

The Ladies' Board of Missions consented to receive the funds. The appeal was successful. Contributions flowed in from the St. Lawrence to the Gulf. The freed-women of the South joined their gifts with the wealthy of the cities. The women rallied from the Atlantic to the Pacific, and in many a mission home in the Rocky Mountains earnest prayer accompanied their gifts on Christmas morning for far-off Alaska.

In February I was able to write to the missionaries at Fort Wrangell, who were anxiously waiting the result of the appeal, "God has heard your prayers. The Church is responding nobly. Two thousand five hundred dollars have been received, and more is coming." This sum eventually reached between four and five thousand dollars. The response from the missionaries was what might have been expected. Rev. S. Hall Young wrote:

"FORT WRANGELL, ALASKA, March 11, 1879.

"REV. SHELDON JACKSON, D.D.

"MY VERY DEAR BROTHER : Your letter of February 15th has caused great rejoicing at the mission. It is the king of all the letters we have received. Our hopes now have eagles' wings. God is better than our fears.. The future that this mission merits seems likely now to be at last proximately realized,

And to you, under God, we give hearty thanks as the kind instrument of this change for the better in our prospects. You have our gratitude far beyond any other man. You have proved yourself an unselfish, self-sacrificing, earnest friend of Alaska and its missionaries. We are all your firm and grateful friends, and pray always for your success and welfare "

Mrs. A. R. McFarland wrote :

" There has been a song in my heart ever since the mail arrived with the news of the noble response of the Church to the call in the *Rocky Mountain Presbyterian* for funds to build the ' Home.'

" I felt sure if we trusted him, God would, in his own good time, send us the help we so much needed. We feel that this is the beginning of glorious times for this mission. Suitable buildings for our work will enable us to accomplish so much more for Christ.

" We are very much rejoiced to hear that Dr. Kendall and yourself are proposing to visit this mission. The Lord bring you to us in safety. I wish every Christian could come and see with their own eyes the great destitutions and needs of this field."

Rev. John G. Brady, of Sitka, then in the East, wrote :

" NEW YORK CITY, March 20, 1879.

" DEAR DR. JACKSON : . . . You have done more than any other one in stirring up an interest in Alaska. Dr. Hastings to-day spoke of the time when you had the large map in his church, Nearly all the funds which have been raised must be credited to your zeal. I wish that you had wings like an eagle, that you might soar over the whole of Alaska, and then tell in the *Rocky Mountain Presbyterian* what you saw. Your appeals, I perceive, have come down with trip-hammer force."

These letters were followed by a unanimous vote of thanks from the Presbytery of Puget Sound, the nearest * presbytery to Alaska.

We now return to Mrs. McFarland's letter-history of the mission :

"FORT WRANGELL, ALASKA, Jan. 8, 1879.

" DR. JACKSON.

" DEAR BROTHER : After I had written you last month, a white man killed another in a billiard-saloon. The mob took possession of the murderer, and would have hung him on the spot, but the more thoughtful ones prevented them. They organized a court and gave him a regular trial. He was convicted and sentenced to death. They proceeded at once to erect a gallows in the main street in the village. Hearing that he was to be hung, I felt that, as Mr. Young was away, I must go and see him. He professed great indifference to the future, although I could

---

* By an oversight of the General Assembly of 1876 in constituting the Synod of the Columbia (see pages 75 and 76, Vol. 4, New Series, of Minutes of the Assembly), and defining the boundaries of the several presbyteries thereof, Alaska was left within the bounds of the Synod of the Pacific, where it was placed by the General Assembly of 1870. (See Minutes of Assembly, page 87, Vol. 1, New Series.)

see that it was forced. Twice in the night, however, he sent for me. He was then in great distress of mind, but got no peace. He told me that he had Christian parents (Presbyterian), but that he had not heard a prayer for twenty years until I prayed with him. It was a terrible scene, and completely unnerved me.

"Since the holidays commenced the Indians have had a gay time. We had a Christmas-tree, and it was a perfect success. We numbered the Indians by hundreds, and yet there was something for each one. The fruit of this tree was furnished by Mrs. Young, from things sent by her friends in the East.

"At midnight the Indians came and sang in front of our houses, and gave us their Christmas salutation. At ten o'clock A.M. they had a procession and hand-shaking. At half-past eleven A.M. we had a Christmas sermon. at tne close of which Mr. Young married one of my pupils to Matthew, our good Indian. Immediately after came the wedding-feast, which was a grand affair for this section.

"During the week there was another wedding and feast, besides several feasts without weddings. Now two white men are soon to wed Indian girls. Thus a very different state of things is springing up here.

"The Home is getting along nicely—that is, if you can call it nice to be getting deeper and deeper in debt every day. I believe it is God's work and that he will raise up the means. And while I feel that faith is an excellent thing to have, yet I am greatly pressed to find anything to eat for these hungry girls. I am very anxious to know the result of your

ARRIVAL OF AN ORGAN.

appeal. The year for the lease of this building is rapidly passing away, and if we are to get up another building in time, we must soon be at work. If we fail to do this, I do not like to think of the consequences."

"FORT WRANGELL, ALASKA, Feb. 11, 1879.

"DEAR BROTHER : The school is very full, and the attendance of the Indians upon church is increasing.

"The Home is prospering beyond my expectations. I now have seven young girls. This week two more applied for admission, but I have to put them off. I could fill the house before sunset, but have to move slowly. We can only enlarge as the Church furnishes the money. The missionary-boxes have been a great help. The girls look so pretty and comfortable in their new dresses. They are so thankful.

" Our organ has arrived in good condition, and is a very great help to us. I am exceedingly anxious to hear about the building fund. Surely such appeals cannot go unheeded."

" March, 1879.—One of my girls has been very sick the past month. It is too bad not to have a physician here. I feel it more than ever now that I have these children to take care of. I hope a teacher may come soon, as Mr. Young is burdened with the school in addition to all his other labors. It was a good providence that sent him to this mission.

" I hope some time this summer to be able to visit Fort Simpson and Metlahkatlah and learn how they carry on their schools. Their experience and methods might assist me. It is after midnight, and I must rest. My correspondence has become a serious matter, and increases every month. Last mail I sent out thirty-five letters. I have already written twenty-eight for this mail, and am not near through yet. My stationery and postage are quite an item."

"April, 1879.—I have taken two more girls into the Home since I last wrote you. One is the daughter of a Tacou shaman or medicine-man. She is twelve years old, and exceptionally pretty and bright. I saw her on the street, and knew that with her winning face she was not safe. My heart went out to her, and I concluded to try and make room for her in my little household.

"Being too unwell to go myself, Mr. Young kindly consented to secure her for me. Taking Mrs. Dickinson, the interpreter, and the little girl, they went in a canoe to where her parents were staying. They had a long wa-wa (talk) before her parents would give her up. But they finally consented, and Mr. Young brought her back with him. I have named her Annie Graham.

"The other girl is only ten years old. But young as she is, her mother had already sold her for ten blankets to a Chilcat Indian for his wire. She was keeping the girl until he brought the blankets. While waiting, the mother was taken sick. An older sister, who does not live at home, hearing of it, brought the child to me. The little girl seems to be perfectly happy with me. She was in great terror of being taken up into the Chilcat country. I have named her Alice Kellogg.

"Rev. S. S. Haury and an assistant, John Baer, both of the Mennonite Church, came up on this steamer and preached for us yesterday morning. We were pleased with him. They have gone on to Sitka and Kadiak. Truly yours,

"A. R. McFarland."

"FORT WRANGELL, ALASKA, May, 1879.

"DEAR BROTHER: We are all rejoiced at the prospect of seeing your party at an early day. The coming of such dear friends will make it seem almost like the East. I feel quite impatient to see a beginning made on our new home. There is now an additional reason for making haste.

"The Roman Catholics are invading our ground. Among the passengers on the Olympia a week ago was a Romish bishop and priest. They at once established a mission. The bishop made an attack on Mr. Young the following Sabbath morning. He was trying to get the people to make the sign of the cross, but none would respond save Shus-taks, the wicked chief. This made the bishop angry, and he broke out as follows : ' Why don't you do as I told you ? Are you afraid of Mr. Young? You are not Mr. Young's slaves. He is not a true minister anyway. No man can be a true minister and have a wife. Look at me ; I am a true minister ; I am all the same as Jesus Christ, and I don't have any wife. By and by Mr. Young will want you to pay lots of money for his wife,' and much more of the same kind.

"The Indians are so fond of outside display and show that the Romish Church would suit them in that respect. But we can take courage as we remember that the Lord is on our side.

"The Home is prospering. The village is crowded with miners, many of them being of the worst kind. If the friends of the mission were here now they would realize more than ever the necessity of protecting the girls. It makes me very happy to feel that at least those in my family are safe. I see that there has been some fault-finding because I took such young girls into the Home. If they who find fault were only here they would see the wisdom of our course. The last girl I received was only ten years old, yet her mother had already sold her to a man for ten blankets."

"June 9th, 1879.—Since writing you last month I have taken three girls into the Home. One is a very bright and pretty child from the Hydah tribe. The other two are half-breed Stickeens. One is seventeen years old.

"Hers is a peculiar case. She lived with an aunt, who was living with a white man. Lately the white man conceived a great fancy for the girl, and has importuned her to live with him, saying that he would send the old woman away. The girl utterly refused to consent to any such thing. The man being called away from home on business, the girl fled to me for protection. She is quite intelligent, speaks English well, and is the best educated Indian in the village. She is very fair, and would pass for a white girl. These make twelve girls now under my care.

"Truly yours. A. R. McFarland."

In June, 1879, Rev. W. H. R. Corlies, M.D., wife and child, of Philadelphia. reached Fort Wrangell.

They had gone out, independent of mission societies, to establish a mission at their own charges. After canvassing the field it was deemed best for Mr. Corlies to settle at Fort Wrangell as a missionary physician. Mrs. Corlies opened a school among the visiting Indians, who in large numbers come to the village for the purpose of trade, and usually camp on the beach above the town.

This school has been very successful, and from it the leaven of the Gospel has been carried to many distant tribes.

During our stay at Wrangell a great medicineman came from the interior, north of the Chilcat country, who had never before seen a white man. He regularly attended church and Sabbath-school, and also Mrs. Corlies' day-school. When the time came for him to return home, he asked Mrs. Corlies to pray for him, and to pray that God would quickly send a teacher for his people.

On the 21st of July, 1879, a party consisting of Dr. and Mrs. Henry Kendall, Dr. and Mrs. A. L. Lindsley, Miss M. J. Dunbar, my wife and myself reached Fort Wrangell and received a very warm welcome from the missionaries and the native Christians.

This was particularly the case with Dr. Kendall. No late event has so favorably impressed the Indians at Fort Wrangell as this visit of Dr. Kendall. Of commanding personal presence, one of the secretaries of a board that has its thousand men stretching from Alaska to Florida, coming from the shores of a distant ocean to inquire after their welfare, bringing the money to erect the Girls' Industrial

Home, it is no wonder that the Indians recognized him as the "Great Chief." One after another of their chiefs and leading men called to see him and express their pleasure at his visit, one with great earnestness remarking that he had not slept all night for joy. The missionaries, too, hailed his coming with delight. His large experience and wise counsels solved for them many a knotty problem. His patience and kindliness in entering into the details of their difficulties and trials, his large sympathies, greatly endeared him to them ; while his hopefulness encouraged their hearts, strengthened their hands, and stimulated them to fresh zeal in the work.

Sabbath, August 3d, 1879, will ever be a memorable day in the history of Alaska. The Presbyterian Mission, commenced August 10, 1877, by the arrival at Fort Wrangell of Mrs. A. R. McFarland and myself, had made such progress during the two years of its existence that Rev. S. Hall Young, the missionary in charge thought it expedient to form his Christian natives into a church. He had for months been instructing them in a special class as to the nature and duties of church-membership.

The presence of several visiting ministers made a suitable occasion.

On Saturday afternoon, August 2d, Rev. Henry Kendall, D.D., preached the preparatory sermon, after which was held the examination of candidates for church-membership. This examination was had through an interpreter, the candidates being unable to speak English, and the examiners equally unable to speak Thlinket,

THE McFARLAND INDUSTRIAL HOME.

Rev. W. H. R. Corlies, Wife and Boy.   Mrs. A. R. McFarland and Girls.   Rev. S. Hall Young and Wife.
Miss Dunbar.   Mrs. Dickinson (the Indian Interpreter).

CHRISTIAN EXPERIENCE. 233

The services continued from three o'clock P.M. to seven, and, after a short intermission for supper, until eleven P.M.

On Sabbath morning at half-past nine o'clock the church came together for prayer.

At half-past ten A.M. the formal organization of the church was effected. Sermon by Rev. Henry Kendall, D.D., constituting prayer by Rev. Sheldon Jackson, D.D., reception and baptism of members by Rev. S. Hall Young, reading of the Covenant by Rev. A. L. Lindsley, D.D., and benediction by Rev. W. H. R. Corlies, M.D.

At three P.M. the church met for the celebration of the Lord's Supper, Rev. S. Hall Young presiding.

The opening prayer was by Dr. Corlies, the address by Dr. Jackson, the distribution of the elements by Dr. Kendall, prayer of thanksgiving by Rev. Mr. Young, and benediction by Dr. Lindsley.

At 7.30 P.M. I preached to the whites, and was followed with an address by Dr. Kendall.

Twenty-three members were received into the new organization, of whom eighteen were Indians, and all of the eighteen, save one, received Christian baptism. The following Sabbath five more were received, four of whom were Indians.

Among the six whites received into membership were Mrs. McFarland and Mrs. Vanderbilt, from the Presbyterian Church of Portland, Oregon; Mrs. Young, from North Granville, N. Y.; Miss Dunbar, from Steubenville, Ohio, and Mr. Regner and Mr. Chapman (two carpenters working upon the church and Home) upon profession of their faith,

It will be of interest to the many friends of the Alaska Mission to know something of the testimony of the native Christians who were received into church-membership. Some of the converts that I found at Fort Wrangell in 1877, as the result of Clah's preaching, had shown that they were not truly regenerated. Others had remained steadfast, and under the instructions of Mrs. McFarland and Rev. Mr. Young had grown in the divine life.

These latter, with others that have been more directly the fruit of Mr. Young's ministry, gave the following testimony, Mrs. Dickinson interpreting :

MOSES LOUIE.—" I am a sinner—very evil. My hope is that God had sent his Son to wash away my guilt. I believe that God has given me a new heart. I love to pray daily for strength. I want only one mind toward Christians."

MARTHA (wife of Moses).—" I have learned about God and Christ, and want them to have pity on me. Will try to obey God as long as I live, not in my own strength, but pray ,God for strength. Daily pray God to have pity on me."

MATTHEW SHAKATS.—" Formerly blind in sin. Very long time in sin. Think God has changed my heart, and I want to come out on God's side. I have had much trouble, and want the help of the Church and of God. Learned of God that Jesus died for me. Now carry my sins to God, and have hope."

AARON KOHANOW.—" I understand very solemn thing to join the church. Indians don't understand as well as white men about it. Willing to go on looking to God to help me. Understand how Christ has spoken that I must be born again. I want the new birth. I ask God to give me a new heart. God hear me. Take my sins and troubles to God." (Aaron was formerly a shaman and sorcerer. Upon his conversion destroyed all the implements of his sorcery.)

ANNIE (Aaron's wife).—" I was sick and told God. I wanted to walk with God's people. Always bal before, because I did not know about God. Now I know about him and want to follow him. The Lord Jesus knows that I am a sinner and he died for me."

JONATHAN KATANAKE (leading councillor of the head chief).—" Willing to try and obey God. Know how God pity on us. Died for me—pains for my sins—pities me, and teaches me to live aright. I try to do it. I give my heart to him. I do not disbelieve about God—how he saved me—I know it. I nearly lost. He stretched out his hand and pulled me back. I feel it. Willing to leave all earthly things. I want to live as God says. Not my strength, only if God helps. Don't say this to make men believe. God knows my heart. I want to live in his sight. When a boy I went to Victoria and heard some one say the Son of God die for people's sins. I did not know then. When sickness come, then I ask the Son of God to save me. Did not ask that sickness go away, but that he save me. God heard me, therefore I believe."

JOHN KADISHAN (chief).—" Yes, true. The Lord die for us. Why disbelieve, when he suffered all pains for us. He came for our sins. I know it when a boy, but did not take it in my heart. Now I take it in. Bible tells us one brother, one heart. I try to love all who love Jesus. Try to love my brothers and sisters—to live straight. God's Spirit now in me. I know it. I believe it with all my heart. When I first go to hear Mr. Young I hear the truth. I fight against it. Temptation hold me back. But I couldn't stand it longer. I must go and talk with Mr. Young. I fight the truth no more. Now I love the truth."

LENA QUONKAH (wife of John).—"When Clah was here he stay at our house. I go to hear him preach. He pray, and get what he prayed for. Then I thought I pray too. God heard me; then I was happy. I like to quit all my badness and give it to Christ, and he take it. I like to live as a Christian —help the poor, pity the sick. I came to tell all my heart before these gentlemen. I tell it all to God."

ISAAC KASCH.—"I came to Mr. Young first time last winter and say I wanted to be his friend and the friend of God. People say you turn your heart to God and laugh at me. I say nobody's business what I do. I mean to serve God. Long ago we blind— all in darkness. We call the crows, and fish, and everything God. But God pity us and give us daylight. He don't want us to die all together. He pity us. Not hard for me to believe in God—that Jesus is the Son of God. I feel different in my heart. My old-fashioned heart was different. I feel my heart is clean now. I live different. I quit all earthly things. I try to do right and pray God. I want to be swift in God's way."

JEREMIAH O'UNK.—"I love God and want to be a Christian. When young, my hair was black, and I never heard of God. Now I am getting old—my hair is white, and I hear about God, and want to love him and obey him. One time I heard about God. Fort Simpson people say, believe God and I would be saved. I try to believe him. I give my heart to God, and want to do what is right. I am a sinner. I always before do bad toward God, but when I heard that Jesus die for my sins, I believe. Formerly I talk bad and strike my wife and children. Now I try to do right, and I pray God to help me do right."

TOY-A-ATT (chief).—"How many sins we must quit on earth! The serpent, he make us blind. That the reason we live so poor. Now God show himself to us and we believe. You know all about how I formerly lived. How I was all the time in trouble and quarreling—all the time when the ball or knife go through me. Now I quit it all. Jesus help me. I live peaceably. I always ask God give me a new heart. Bible tells how Jesus lived on earth—not proud. The Son of God, he washed his disciples' feet. I wash all the brethren's feet. Two things I want: Be like little children; thank God help us always. Formerly I love myself. Didn't want to die quick—all blind heart. Now I know better, and want to love every one. I love my enemies, and pray God to save them. I see many children. I pray God send ministers and teachers. God hear my prayer. I very happy."

MARY KATLSEEH.—"Like to be a church-member

because God die for my sins on the cross. That is the reason I like to pray God. I do not put my face before any people. God knows my heart. I want to serve him."

MARY FLANERY.—"I like to love my Saviour and give all my badness to him, tell him all my sins, carry my heavy-laden to him, and ask him to forgive all my sins. I am willing, and want to love God with all my heart. Nobody tell me about him until Mr. Young come. I now believe him."

Mrs. JENNIE CHURCH.—"I believe the Church is God's road, and I want to be in it and love God. I confess my sins before his face. I put them all away. I give myself to God's service."

REBECCA SHETUTAYAH.—"I like to be a friend to Christ. I want to give all my sins to him. I am poor and weak. I believe in God because he shows how he loves me, pities me, and saves me. When I was nearly gone down into the pit of everlasting fire, he pities on me and die to save me. I try to stop all my sins. I don't want to go in the wrong way any more. God shows me what is the right way. I pray him help me."

Mrs. JENNIE STEELE.—"I like to be a church-member. Quit all my sins I used to do before. Because God saved my life, I want to do right and not as I used to do before I give myself to God."

LOT TY-EEN.—"Yes, I feel God's Spirit come to me. I feel how sin I am before. I knew not God then. Now my heart differ. I feel now God forgive my sin. I feel it in my heart that I love God because he save me. I believe Jesus Christ died for me—pay my sin. God teach me to love one another. I try to obey God and love them all. If enemy come to me, I love him, and show him the right, and tell him about God. If he starve, I feed him."

EMMA TY-EEN (Lot's wife).—" I was sinner-full of sin, because I didn't know how to live. God knows it. I now give it all to Jesus. I don't want to hide back my sin. I give it all to Jesus who died for me with nails in his hands and feet, and knife in his side, and that's why I don't want to go back to my sins. I want to live right. I trust Jesus help me. Not my own strength to put away sins. All the things I put behind me. Earthly things like rust in my flesh. I obey my husband, and obey God, and help the poor and sick."

RICHARD KATCHKUKU (married his uncle's wife by inheritance).—" Great sinner—hungry and want something to eat of God's word to satisfy my soul. I hear about God a long while, but did not feel in my heart. Now I feel in my heart, and want to join with my brothers and sisters. God pity me. His spirit come to me. I give all my heart to God. I look to Jesus for help, and ask him to forgive all my sin. I like to tell every one the good news about God."

MARY KATCHKUKU (Richard's wife).—" I like to love Jesus, and that's the reason why I want to come to him. I feel sorry that I always disobey God before, but now I praise my Saviour because he die for me. And I don't like to dirty his face any more. Four years been believing in God, ever since Clah first tell me about him. If in my house, or canoe, or in the woods, wherever I am, always pray to God."

While we were at Fort Wrangell arrangements were made for pushing forward the mission buildings as rapidly as the necessary materials could be procured. The church was to be 36x55 feet in size, and the Girls' Industrial Home 40x60 feet, two stories high, besides attic and basement.

No one that has not tried building a thousand miles from a hardware store and a hundred miles from a saw-mill, in a community where there was not a horse, wagon, or cart, and but one wheelbarrow, can realize the vexatious delays incident to such a work.

Nevertheless the church was completed so as to be occupied for worship on Sabbath, October 5th; and the Home was inclosed, but will not be finished until the spring of 1880. In October Rev. S. Hall Young, accompanied by Professor Muir of California, Toy-a-att and Kadeshan, and two young men, made a canoe voyage up the coast as far as the Chilcat villages to see what could be done toward the establishment of schools among them. We give the following extracts from his report:

"Passing through Kake Strait to its junction with Prince Frederick Sound, we came to the principal Kake town, called Klukquann (no sleep). The village consists of some half dozen large houses and some smaller ones. It is beautifully situated on a charming bay, with a wide, dry, sandy beach. In the immediate neighborhood there is an abundance of good land from which the people raise quantities of potatoes and turnips. Their country is the best adapted for agriculture of any we found on our trip. The tribe numbers three hundred and sixty-four, and has a bad name. Several years ago a party of six white men were murdered by them. We met the principal men. They listened reverently to our message and asked for a teacher. But there was an air of suspicion and indifference among them that we did not find at the other villages. An earnest Christian teacher would not find any difficulty in working a great change among them. A majority of this

SEAL SKIN SHOES.

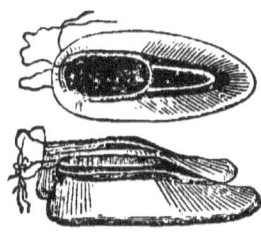
SEAL-SKIN MOCCASINS.

people had never heard the Gospel message before. The nefarious traffic in their women at Fort Wrangell and Sitka and the manufacture and use of *hoochinoo* are making fearful inroads upon their numbers. This village is on the north-west side of Kuprianoff Island. . . . Monday, October 20th, we reached Letushkan, on Admiralty Island, a village of the Hootznahoos. It is a mean, dirty-looking place, of low, dingy houses, and contains a population of two hundred and forty-six. They are very poor and degraded, and their chief said to us with great earnestness that the only hope of saving his people from speedy ruin was in the coming of a missionary ; that whiskey and the debauchery of their women were making fearful ravages among them ; that he and his people would gladly yield obedience to a missionary should one come, and that there would be but little difficulty in suppressing intemperance.

"Tuesday we reached Angoon, the chief town of the Hootznahoos. It is beautifully situated, and has a population of four hundred and ten. But we did not remain long, as the whole town was drunk.

"We next visited Kowdekan, the large village of the Hoonyah tribe. It is located on a beautiful deep bay on the north-east shore of Tchitchagoff Island. The population is six hundred and twenty-five. They are a simple-hearted, primitive people. The women are comparatively unpolluted, and the children numerous. They have constant communication by canoe with Sitka and Fort Wrangell. We should make this one of our chain of mission stations among the Thlinket-speaking people. . . .

"Gayrun is the lower village of the Chilcats, at the mouth of Chilcat River (pronounced by the natives Chitl Kawt). We were met at the landing with the firing of guns and great demonstrations of joy. At a subsequent conference, Kath, the chief, speaking for the people, expressed their great satisfaction at the prospect of a missionary being sent to them ; that it was what they had been asking for a long time ; that, from what they had seen at Fort Wrangell of the fruits of Christianity, they had been led already to give up a belief in their old superstitions, and were ready to adopt the religion of the white

INDIANS GAMBLING.

men, who excelled them in every branch of knowledge.

" They offered to donate a large new house to the missionary for church and school purposes.

" I never before saw a people so hungry for the word of God. They filled the house of the chief, where we spoke, to suffocation, and some who could not get in climbed upon the roof and listened through the aperture for the escape of the smoke, enduring the cold for two hours at a time rather than miss any of our message. When we were through they refused to go away, saying, ' Your words are food to our hearts,' and insisting that we should preach again and again. They are a fine-looking, intelligent people. Many are rich, and nearly all in comfortable circumstances. They control the trade of a large tract of country inland, and are sharp traders. The women are virtuous, and seem to have at least as much honor from the men as they show to their husbands. They are far from being slaves. I noticed that all the hard work, such as getting wood, carrying water, and caring for the canoes, was done by the men, and indeed a good deal of housework is done by them also.

" Children swarm about every house. Their old laws are in force, but the superstitions which answer for their religion are held very slightly. An old medicine-man who was present said that when the missionary came he would cut his hair and cease his sorceries. We were unable to reach the principal village, twenty-five miles up the river, on account of a severe storm and the lateness of the season. Shathitch, the chief, sent down a canoe for us. I would like nothing better than to enter such a place as a pioneer missionary, and see what could be done toward lifting up to a high standard of Christian civilization a naturally noble people. I know of no other place where, so far as we can judge, such valuable results could be achieved by the same amount of effort in so short a time.

"On the eastern side of Admiralty Island we visited the village of Auke. They were the most degraded, poverty-stricken, brutal people we visited. Many of them were half drunk. In several of their camps we found *hoochinoo* stills at work making rum. We reached Fort Wrangell upon our return, November 21st, and found that the work had progressed beyond our hopes. Several accessions are expected at our next communion. The incidental expenses of the church are now all provided for by the Indians. The congregations number from two hundred to three hundred. The Sabbath-school has an average attendance of one hundred and seventy-five, with six teachers. The home is very prosperous."

Mrs. McFarland writes:

"FORT WRANGELL, ALASKA, Oct. 11, 1879.

"DEAR BROTHER: Our church last Sabbath was largely attended. In the evening there was a larger congregation of whites than I have ever before seen at this place. Mr. Young preached an excellent sermon from the text, 'I would rather be a doorkeeper,' etc.

"Miss Dunbar is proving herself a very competent and efficient teacher in the school.

"Tillie has broken her engagement with the young Indian. She concludes she could not marry an unbeliever. She says, 'John does not care anything about God, while I am trying to be a Christian, and I know I would not be happy with him. He would only drag me down again to be a "*siwash*" (degraded heathen woman). I asked her why she had promised to marry him. She replied, 'I never wanted him. It was my family made the match.' I then inquired if she preferred any other, to which she replied, 'No, I want to stay with you, for I fear I cannot be good if I am not where I can have your assistance.'. The young man is very angry, and threatens that she shall not marry any one else.

"We have now divided the Sabbath-school into five classes. Miss Dunbar has all the girls who can read in the Testament. Dr. Corlies has the boys who can read. Mrs. Corlies and Mrs. Chapman have the little ones. I have the larger girls and women who can not read, and Mr. Young takes the larger boys and men. This will be a great improvement on the time when I had them all in a class together. Truly yours,
"A. R. McFARLAND."

Miss Dunbar writes :

"FORT WRANGELL, ALASKA, October 11, 1879.

"DEAR SIR : I have opened my school with forty-five scholars ; have been teaching three weeks. I think I shall like it very much indeed. My time is so busily occupied that it passes very quickly. I have school five hours, and from four to six we study the language with Mrs. Dickinson. It is very hard. We are now translating the first chapter of Genesis. I am taking music lessons from Mrs. Young; practice one hour and a half before school. There is an organ in the school-room, and I find it very convenient. Friday afternoon we devote to knitting, plain sewing and patch-work, singing, etc., etc. The large boys saw enough wood to last the coming week. Classes range from A B C to fourth reader, geography, and practical arithmetic. I find the Indians quite as ready to learn as the white children, and not half so mischievous. The Indians are now coming home from their fishing and hunting grounds, and this winter we will have a large school. I am training some of the larger girls to assist me with the small children. Mothers and daughters stand side by side in class, and it is interesting to see what delight they take in turning one another down in spelling-class. The children are very fond of singing. Some have very sweet voices. They would all be so proud to have a singing-book of their own. The girls are learning to do housework. They wash and iron quite well, and the oldest girl is a nice baker. We all eat at the same time, but have separate tables from the girls. When they are excused, each girl carries her own plate, cup and saucer to the kitchen, and the table is cleared off very quietly and quickly. They make quite a business of eating—do not talk much at the table—and do you believe it? these girls never knew what it was to eat at a table before they came into the Home.

"Now I will tell you how we spend Sabbath. It

is the busiest day in the week. Preaching at ten o'clock, Sunday-school at close of church. Preaching again at three o'clock in the afternoon, sometimes in Chinook, but often through an interpreter in the Stickeen language. In the evening preaching in English for the whites. We look forward to this service with pleasure, as the other services are necessarily very tedious. In the evening before church the children in the Home recite the catechism and Scripture verses. We have worship at our meals before we begin to eat. In the evening the girls come into my room to read a chapter before they retire. They read quite well now.

" From my room the view is exquisite, overlooking the bay. At a distance you can see the snow-capped peaks. One mountain after another rises out of the sea like domes. This is a wonderful country. God has done much to beautify it.

" The names of our girls, from the smallest to the largest, are Nellie, Fannie, Susie, Mary Jackson, Hattie, Louisa Norcross, Annie Graham, Kitty, Alice Kellogg, Emma, Katie, Minnie, Eliza, Johanna, Tillie Kinnou. Truly yours,

" MAGGIE J. DUNBAR."

"FORT WRANGELL, ALASKA, November 11, 1879.

" DEAR BROTHER : My family has increased very much since you were here. I now report twenty girls. This greatly increases my cares. Last Sabbath Dr. Corlies suggested at the morning service that some of the Christian Indians should go up the beach, where a number of heathen Indians were encamped, and invite them to church in the afternoon. This was done, and resulted in the church being crowded to overflowing. There was not even standing room left. It was very inspiring to see so many of those poor creatures, with their blankets and painted faces, crowding into the church. We earnestly pray that it may be the beginning of a revival among us. Truly yours,

"MRS. A. R. McFARLAND."

"FORT WRANGELL, ALASKA, Nov. 29, 1879.

"DEAR SIR : . . . The school is prosperous and every department of the mission flourishing. The great eagerness of this people to receive instruction is wonderful. I was told before coming here that the Indians could not learn. But in this respect I have been very agreeably disappointed. I must say that in dress, order, and studiousness they rank with many of our common schools. In singing, reading, spelling, writing, at the blackboard or mental arithmetic, they evince ability to learn what white children learn. Perhaps they are a little slower, but considering that they are mastering a new language at the same time, all due allowance can be made for them. The days are so short we are obliged to have only one session of the school. It extends from ten A.M. until half-past two P.M., without any intermission. Mr. Young has reopened the night-school for those who cannot attend during the day. Dr. Corlies and Mr. Chapman are assisting him. Our oldest girl in the Home (Tillie Kinnou) has become a Christian, and expresses a great desire to be trained for a teacher. She is already quite a help in teaching the younger children. She is a girl of much promise and decision of character.

"Mrs. Corlies is doing a great work among the wild Indians. Many of their children attend church and Sabbath-school. We are thankful for the prayers of God's dear people. With God's favor and blessing we can build up a model Christian village that shall reflect light and radiate heat to many darkene(tribes all along this coast. Truly yours,

"MAGGIE J. DUNBAR."

"FORT WRANGELL, ALASKA, December 16, 1879.

"DEAR BROTHER: The mission work here is in a very prosperous condition.

"The new church is filled at every service. The Roman Catholics are making very little headway, and the priest has gone down to Victoria.

"About the middle of November we organized a woman's prayer-meeting. We meet every Friday afternoon, and have an attendance of from 25 to 30 Every Indian woman present who is a church-member leads in prayer. We expect much good from these meetings.

"Miss Dunbar's school is very full and prosperous. She is an excellent teacher.

"The Home is doing well. It is a bright, cheerful, and happy family of 20 girls. The poor little girl whom I received while you was here, whose mother was murdered, is a delicate child, and I fear may not live long.

"Nothing has been done with the murderer. The

Indians have been waiting for all the principal men to return to the village. This week they have had a council and determined to arrest and try the man. If he is found guilty they will probably execute him.

"We have had two weeks of cold weather, the severest I have felt since coming to Fort Wrangell.

"This house is so cold that we could not keep comfortable. During this cold spell all my house plants were frozen. Next to my work, I loved them better than anything else in Alaska.

"Dr. Corlies has moved into his new house near the church.

"Mrs. Corlies' school for the visiting Indians is quite large. The transient character of the pupils, as they come and go with their parents, makes it very hard and discouraging. But she has such lovely faith that she labors on cheerfully, ever hoping that they may carry to their own tribes some seed that will yet bear fruit. As Christmas draws near the Indians are all excitement. This is the greatest day of the year for them. Through the kindness of many friends in the East, we will have a nice Christmas-tree.

"I send most heartfelt thanks to all the dear friends East and West for their many gifts. I am sure they would feel amply repaid if they could witness the pleasure they afford these poor people. May God bless them all for their kindness to us. Many of the packages have nothing about them by which we can learn the donors. I thank them all the same, and commend them to the Saviour, who knows their gift of love.

"For a long time I have been trying to get into the Home the little daughter of Shus-Staaks, the wicked chief who once threatened my life.

"Yesterday he sent the child to me, saying that he was a wicked old man himself, but he wanted his little girl to be good, and he wanted Mrs. McFarland to teach her. She is a nice child, about 13 years old, and I have named her Louisa Norcross, Shus-Staaks.

"We are very much rejoiced at this, as the old chief has opposed our work from the beginning, and been the chief supporter of the Roman Catholic movement. He now attends our church regularly.

"We are also rejoicing in the hope that Chief Shaaks is a converted man. He has asked to be baptized and received into church-membership. I received sixty-six letters by this steamer.

"Sincerely yours,
"Mrs. A. R. McFarland."

The year 1879 closed with the re-establishment of the school at Sitka, the arranging of missions among the Chilcats, Hydahs, and Hoonyahs, and great prosperity at Fort Wrangell.

ALASKA DOG-HEAD.

CHAPTER IX.

A Canoe Voyage—Deserted Indian Village—Toiling in Rowing—Councils with Chilcats, Hydas, and Tongas—New Fields—Fort Tongas—Driving before the Storm—An Indian Welcome.

"Angel of life ! thy glittering wings explore
Earth's loneliest bounds and ocean's wildest shore.
Now far he sweeps, where scarce a summer smiles,
On Bering's rocks, or Greenland's naked isles."

I HAD long wanted to make a visit to the missions of the Methodist and Episcopal Churches at Fort Simpson and Metlahkatlah, and inspect their plans and methods of labor. The latter of these missions has been in operation twenty years, and sufficient time (an important element in mission work) has elapsed to test the efficiency of their methods. Besides, these missions were the forerunner of our own work in Alaska. Unable to visit them in any other way, I concluded, during my visit to Alaska in 1879, to make the trip in a canoe. Just at that time a large one came in from the Chilcat country, loaded with furs and bound for Fort Simpson. As a portion of the crew were Christian Indians from Fort Simpson, there was no difficulty in arranging a passage. Besides the six Christian Indians, there were twelve wild Chilcat savages, headed by two chiefs, one of whom was a medicine-man or shaman.

A DESERTED VILLAGE.

The canoe was about thirty-five feet long, five wide, and three deep. A comfortable seat was allotted me in the centre, with my blanket and provisions within easy reach. On the 11th of August we left Fort Wrangell for Fort Simpson and Metlahkatlah, B. C. The day wore on with the monotonous dip of the paddles. Rounding a cape, they were able to hoist two sails, and have their assistance for a short distance.

Late in the afternoon we passed an abandoned Stickeen village. A number of the ancient *totem* poles were still standing, surmounted by grotesque images, and containing the bones and ashes of the former inhabitants. Many had fallen and are rotting amid the dense undergrowth of bushes and ferns. Some of the corner-posts of their large houses were still standing, resting upon the top of which are immense beams, some of them three feet through and from forty to sixty feet long.

Without an inhabitant, the coarse croaking of the raven alone broke in upon the stillness and desolation of the scene. The Indians, resting upon their paddles, gazed intently at the ruins as we floated by with the tide. What thoughts were passing through their minds I had no means of knowing. Perhaps the savage Chilcats looked upon the scene with superstitious dread and awe, while to the Christian Tsimpseans (Simp-se-ans) it brought joy and gratitude as they more fully realized that the heathen darkness of the past had been changed to light and hope.

If those ruins had a voice to rehearse the scenes that

have passed within them, the whole Christian world would stand aghast and horrified at the cruelties which it is possible for human nature to enact and even gloat over. When those great corner-posts were placed in position, a slave was murdered and placed under each. When the houses were completed and occupied, scores of slaves were butchered, to show the power and wealth of the owner—that his slaves were so numerous that he could afford to kill, and yet have plenty left. Founded and dedicated with human sacrifices, who can conceive of the aggregate of woe and suffering in those habitations of cruelty, year after year, at the wild, drunken orgies of the Indians—their horrid cannibal feasts, their inhuman torture of witches, their fiendish carousals around the burning dead, the long despairing wails of lost souls as they passed out into eternal darkness? They have passed away to meet us at the judgment-seat, and their village is in ruins. But other villages exist on this coast, where these same scenes of cruelty and blood are still enacted. When will the Christian Church awake to its responsibility, and send the light into all this benighted land?

Frequently along the way the Chilcat Indians would break out into singing one of their national airs, to cheer the rowers. This would challenge the Christian Indians, who would follow with a number of the precious hymns of Bliss and Sankey. One evening, after a large number of these had been sung, the old Chilcat and shaman inquired, "Who is this Jesus you sing about?" Then the Tsimpsean Indians gladly preached Jesus unto him.

A SCALP DANCE.

1

These Christian Indians carry their religion with them wherever they go. They were now returning from a voyage of over a thousand miles. They had been on the way for weeks. But under no circumstances would they travel on the Sabbath. Upon one occasion they were nearly out of food, and their heathen companions urged them to continue the voyage, that they might reach an Indian village and procure supplies. The heathen said, "We are hungry, and you are no friends of ours if you do not go where we can get something to eat." But neither tide, wind, nor hunger could induce them to travel on the Lord's day. One of them afterward said, in a meeting of his own people, that his heart was often sad upon the trip because he did not know more of the language of the people they were visiting, and could not tell them more about Jesus.

It is the universal testimony of the whites, both friends and foes of the missions, that the Christian Indians of Metlahkatlah, Fort Simpson, and Fort Wrangell are strict in the observance of the Sabbath.

I was much interested in my Chilcat companions, and, like the Christian Indians, deplored that I could not more fully communicate with them. However, after we reached Fort Simpson, where an interpreter could be had, they came and sought a council. The two chiefs, speaking in behalf of their people, declared their desire to give up the old way and learn the new, which was better; that they were ready and waiting to give up their heathen practices, as soon as a teacher would come and show them how, and they earnestly inquired *how soon* a teacher would come. These people occupy the country at the head of Lynn Channel, and were known to the Hudson Bay Fur Company, at an early day, as the Nehaunees. They are a bold, warlike, and enterprising people. They are also noted traders, being the middle-men between the interior tribes and the American merchants on the coast. They number about two thousand.

I promised to present their case to the Board, and encouraged them to believe that a missionary would be sent. These were the people that we had hoped to visit in their northern homes, but being prevented from reaching them, they were thus providentially sent to us. The Rev. Mr. Young, of Fort Wrangell, and the Rev. J. G. Brady, of Sitka, have had frequent conferences with members of this tribe, and concur in the importance of establishing a mission among them at an early day.

I also had a council with some Hydahs. We camped one night on their island. They re-echoed the universal desire of the people along this coast for schools, and I promised to bring their case also before the board.

At Fort Simpson I was visited by a delegation of Tongas, who had the same request to make for help. I could only promise to try and interest the Church in their behalf. The Indians think that the whites have some great secret about the future state of the soul, which they wish to learn. They are in a condition of expectancy which would cause them warmly to welcome Christian teachers. But if this season is permitted by the Church to pass away unimproved, who can say that it will not be followed by greater hardness of heart and more determined heathenism?

About six P.M. the canoe was run upon the beach, and an hour spent in supper, which, to the Indians, consisted of tea and salmon. Embarking at seven, they paddled until ten o'clock, when, finding an opening in the rock-bound coast, we put ashore, spread our blankets upon the sand, and were soon sound asleep. At three A.M. we were roused and were soon under way, without any breakfast. This, however, did not matter much, as my stock of provisions consisted of ship biscuit and smoked salmon. Biscuit and salmon for breakfast and supper, salmon and biscuit for dinner. The Indians upon the trip only averaged one meal the twenty-four hours.

During the morning, passing the mouth of a shallow mountain stream, the canoe was anchored to a big rock. The Indians, wading up the stream, in a few minutes, with poles and paddles clubbed to death some thirty salmon, averaging twenty-five pounds each in weight. These were thrown into the canoe and taken along.

At noon they put ashore for their first meal that day. Fires were made under shelter of a great rock. The fish, cleaned and hung upon sticks, were soon broiling before the fire. After dinner all hands took a nap upon the beach. At three P.M. we were again under way. When night came, finding no suitable landing-place, the Indians paddled on until two o'clock next morning, having made a day's work of twenty-three hours. At two A.M., finding a sheltered bay, we ran ashore. As it was raining hard, we spread our blankets as best we could, under sheltering rocks or projecting roots of the great pines.

At six o'clock, rising from an uncomfortable sleep,

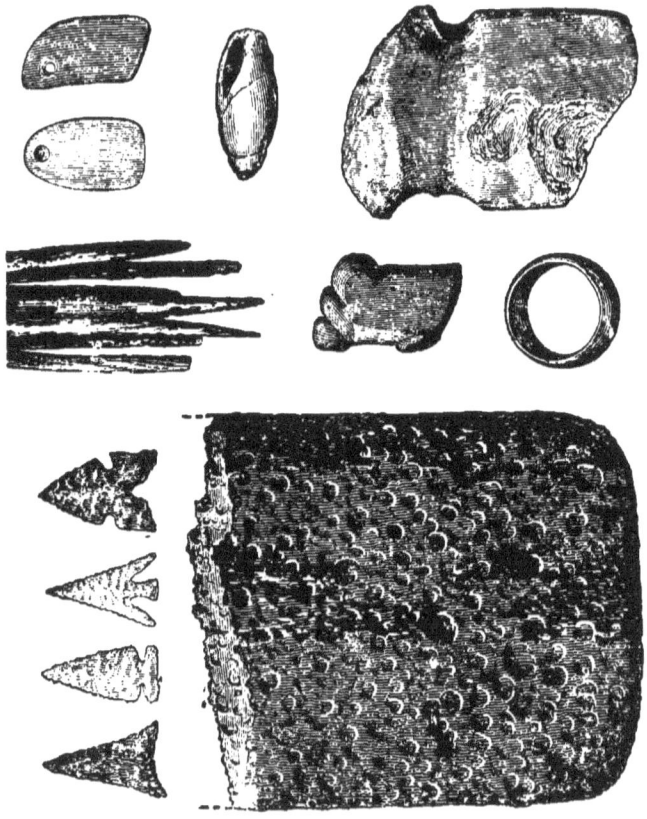

STONE IMPLEMENTS.

we embarked and paddled until nine, when, reaching the cabin of Mr. Morrison, at Tongas Narrows, we went ashore for breakfast. Mr. Morrison has a fine vegetable garden, and is also engaged in salmon fisheries. At this point I secured two fine specimens of stone axes.

In an hour we were again under way, the Indians working hard at the paddles until the middle of the afternoon, when we ran ashore upon a rocky point for a short rest and sleep, the sea being very rough.

In an hour and a half we were again on our journey. Toward evening we passed Cape Fox and boldly launched out to cross an arm of the sea, and once out it was as dangerous to turn back as to go forward. The night was dark, the waves rolling high, and the storm upon us. One Indian stood upon the prow of the canoe watching the waves and giving orders. Every man was at his place, and the stroke of the paddles kept time with the measured song of the leader, causing the canoe to mount each wave with two strokes; then, with a click, each paddle would, at the same instant, strike the side of the canoe and remain motionless, gathering strength for the next wave. As the billows struck the canoe it quivered from stem to stern.

It was a long, tedious night, as in the rain and fog and darkness we tossed in a frail canoe upon the waters, but daylight found us near Fort Tongas.

This is an Indian village and an abandoned military post. From the water there seemed to be a whole forest of crest or *totem* poles. Many of them are from sixty to seventy-five feet high, and carved from top to bottom with a succession of figures representing the eagle, wolf, bear, frog, whale, and other animals. The military post was established in

1867 and abandoned in 1877. The buildings are still standing. The chief has repeatedly, in a most earnest and urgent manner, asked for a teacher for his people before, through the combined effect of vice and whiskey, they become extinct.

The wind had been against us all the way from Fort Wrangell. It had rained more or less each day that we had been out, and the storm had continued to increase in violence. Some of the Indians being so exhausted by the labors of the past night that they dropped asleep at their paddles, it was thought best to go ashore and get some rest. On shore we tried to start a fire, but the driving rain soon extinguished it. Taking my regulation meal of salmon and hard-tack, I spread my blankets under a big log and tried to sleep. The beating storm soon saturated the blankets, and I awoke to find the water running down my back. Rising, I paced up and down the beach until the Indians were ready to move on. After a rest of two hours, seeing no signs of a lull in the storm, we re-embarked, determined, if possible, to make Fort Simpson.

Getting out of the shelter of the island into Dixon's Inlet (another arm of the ocean), we found the wind in our favor. Hoisting both sails, we drove through the waves at a slashing rate, the corner of the sails dipping into the water, and occasionally the waves running over the side into the canoe. This was fun for the Indians, who would again and again exclaim, as our masts bent under the sails, "Beat steamboat! beat steamboat!" Cold, wet, and hungry, that afternoon we ran into the harbor at Fort Simpson, and

AN INDIAN WELCOME. 265

shortly after were receiving a warm welcome at Rev. Thomas Crosby's mission of the Methodist Church of Canada.

In the spring I had written to the Rev. Thomas Crosby that the Rev. Henry Kendall, D.D., one of the secretaries of the Presbyterian Board of Home Missions, and myself would visit Alaska in July, and if possible would call at his mission.

The announcement of this created great joy among the Indians. Consequently, in July they came home from their fisheries to the number of over one thousand, and festooned the principal streets of their village with evergreens from one end to the other.

Their flags were ready and their cannon in position to welcome the "great white chiefs of missions." But, to our great disappointment, circumstances prevented our landing. When, therefore, they heard that I had arrived by canoe, a meeting of the chiefs and councilmen was called to give a public welcome.

Being all assembled at the council chamber in the mission-house, Moses McDonald, a chief, rose and addressed me in substance thus, Mr. Crosby interpreting :

" Your coming has made our hearts very happy. We expected you before. Our people came in and made great preparations. We festooned our streets in your honor, but you did not come. Our flowers and evergreens faded ; our people went back to their fisheries. But though now, because our people are away, we cannot make as much demonstration, our hearts are just as much glad.

" We are glad that you are coming to help the

poor people, our neighbors, the Stickeens. When we hear of the great American nation—its large cities, its great business houses, its vast wealth and churches—we are amazed that you did not do something for this people a long time ago. We hope you will tell your people about it strong. We hope you will have whiskey put down. We have put it down here, and it can be put down there.

"We do not think it well to have two (denominations) churches among the Stickeens. The Stickeens ought to speak strong all the one way. We hope your missionary, Mr. Young, will be strong everywhere—directing about the streets and houses and good order and sick, every day. We hope he will keep the people driving on—all warm. All the work you see here has been done in five years. It could not have been done if the missionary had not worked very hard and all the time to show us how to work. Indians are different from white men. They need a minister to lead them.

"All I have to say is this, that a good man be sent to our neighbors, the Tongas. The way is open. If you strike now you will get them. They will soon be gone if not rescued."

John Ryan next spoke :

"We are delighted to meet you here. You see the place very quiet, because nobody home. If all home, it is very peaceable, because the peace of Christ has come here. It was not so formerly. This was a great people for darkness and cruelty before the missionary came, and that was but a few years ago. Our hearts were first like the Stickeens'. We thought

AURORA ON THE YUKON RIVER, ALASKA.

the new way was all wrong. But God has conquered and changed the whole life of our people. God pitied us, heard our cry, sent his minister, and built his house. It was God's work. God heard our prayers. Then we prayed for the Stickeens, and God heard and came to their help. That is the way. When we see any one in trouble, we help, we pray.

"If you send only one minister, then the work is heavy, but if you send more it will be light.

"Look! we thought it was only the English and Canadian that loved to help this people, because we saw no one else come. But now we see our American friends come and have warm, strong hearts too. Now we all work together for Christ.

"Last winter we went far off, and carried God's word wherever we went. We did not go to make money or get great names, but to carry the word of God to others. We visited four large villages that asked where the missionary was. We had no authority to tell them that one would come, but we said to them, Tell God your hearts. Pray to him to send a missionary, and one will come."

Samuel Musgrave Gemk was the next speaker. He said :

"I want to tell this chief how glad my heart is that he come to visit our minister. Half of my heart very glad, and half a little sorry. We are a little sorry that you did not wait a little out there on the island, that we might have gone into our boxes and got out our flags and fired our guns, and made you feel very welcome. But we did not know when you were coming, and now we are delighted to see you sitting alongside of our minister. Just one thing I say. Not good as Christians, we be as old, heathens at enmity. Now we like brothers. I wish you would push one part of the country into the other. This line ought to be lost. Hope that it be done, because if one country, then we all brothers. Then be no more English Christians and American Christians, but we will all be one Christians. Then if you need a little help, or we need a little help, we can help each other. Since your minister go to the Stickeens, we feel at home there now. If we get sick or die there, we feel we should be cared for now."

Wicke-tow followed :

" Don't think I am lazy, that I do not stand up to speak, for I am lame (he is partly paralyzed). It was very hard for me to get here, but my heart was so happy because you come that I could not keep away.

" If you had come when we expected you, or if we had had time to get ready now, when you come, it would not be hard to show how we honor you.

" I am not old, but I remember how it was when chiefs of another tribe came. We had great rejoicings, and so we would have done for you if we had known when you were coming. We are sorry that Dr. Kendall is not here with you. That is right, you have come and started in among American Indians. Go on. Don't think that the Tsimpseans were always as now. They were very wicked and dark and bad. How they plunged into all evil ! But God sent Mr. Crosby, and now it is impossible for the devil to succeed. I believe the devil now have to die at Fort Simpson. So it will not be long before the Stickeen people give up the old way. One thing will conquer Indian people sooner than anything. By kindness you can lead them in the new way."

David Swanson said :

" Our hearts are very happy to see you here. When I was a little bo ·, and we were so blind, nobody thought of us. Now we see the great interest other people take in our welfare. Then very few good people ever notice us. Our minister get a letter that you were coming. I think, Why is this ? Why does this man so far off want to see us ? It must be God's work. I am but a young man, but I am astonished at the changes here. Here in a few years all change so fast. Only a few old sticks and old houses left. All change so fast when Jesus come. Surely it must be God's work to change here and put it in people's hearts way off that they want to see us. This makes our hearts very strong to see you. We now believe that other people are thinking and praying for us. We are willing to go where God wants us. We have been over to Tongas, but they say to us, You are English and we are American. We wish you would send them an American preacher. They have a great deal of whiskey at Tongas, and it is bad for them. It was bad for us a few years ago. Now that our hearts are changed, we feel for those people that once were our enemies.

" We see no difference at all between killing men with whiskey and killing them with a gun. It has been put away by us, and it can be put away by your people. Your government has strong arm and can stop it. We could go from here and destroy all of it, but we have no right to do it in your country. If in our country, we would do it, and the people be saved.

"Whiskey has done bad work. Among some tribes only a few left—nearly all gone.

"One year and a half ago we went over to Tongas and preached to the people, and they were all ready for a minister, and now we hope you are going to take hold of it and give them a minister."

After a suitable reply by myself, the council adjourned with prayer and a general shaking of hands.

Just before leaving Fort Simpson I was waited upon by a committee of the council to inquire what more they could do to show their joy at my visit.

After a delightful Sabbath spent with Mr. Crosby and his Indians, I continued my canoe voyage down the coast to visit the celebrated mission of the Church Missionary Society at Metlahkatlah (Met-lah-katlah).

ALASKA SEA-GULL.

CHAPTER X.

Missions of the Church Missionary Society of England in British Columbia on the Border of Alaska—Cannibalism—A Christian Village—Triumphs of Grace—Tradition Concerning the First Appearance of the Whites.

> " Hark the solemn trumpet sounding
> Loud proclaims the jubilee :
> 'Tis the voice of grace abounding,
> Grace to sinners rich and free ;
> Ye who know the joyful sound,
> Publish it to all around."

THERE are few chapters in missionary history more full of romance or more wonderful than those which record the work of God among the native tribes of the North Pacific coast.

On the 2d of May, 1669, Charles II. granted a charter to his cousin, Prince Rupert, conveying the exclusive right to form settlements and carry on trade in the northern regions of this continent. This was the commencement of the famous Hudson Bay Company, whose hardy, adventurous agents penetrated and made known to geographical science almost every portion of the great north-land.

Among the most enterprising of these pioneers was Alexander Mackenzie. In 1793 he had pressed forward to the head waters of Peace River, crossed the summit of the Rocky Mountains, and stood upon the shores of the Pacific Ocean. In 1806 Simon Fraser had crossed the mountains and established a post of the Hudson Bay Company on the Pacific side. And about 1821 Fort Rupert, on Vancouver's Island, and Fort Simpson, on the borders of Alaska, were established. The establishment of these posts called the attention of British Christians to the condition of the Indian tribes, which number in British Columbia over 28,000. These belong to several nations with distinct languages. They are again subdivided into many tribes speaking different dialects.

It was not, however, until 1856 that an effort was made for the establishment of a mission. In that year Captain (now Admiral) Prevost, of the Royal Navy, being ordered to visit that coast, offered a free passage to any person whom the Church Missionary Society would commission. In response to this offer Mr. William Duncan was sent out, arriving at Fort Simpson on the 1st of October, 1857.

Mr. Duncan had been an ordinary clerk in a mercantile establishment. The secretaries of the Church Missionary Society, upon one occasion, had appointed a missionary meeting in the church he attended. When they arrived from London the evening proved so stormy that only nine persons were present as an audience. One of the secretaries recommended dismissing the meeting, but another said, "No; we have come here to hold a missionary service, and I am in favor of holding it." The addresses were made, and at the close of the meeting Mr. Duncan, one of the nine, offered himself as a missionary.

When he announced his purpose to his employers, they tried to dissuade him from going. They offered to increase his salary to one thousand dollars and give him a certain percentage in the sales, that would have made him a wealthy man.

But he could not be turned aside. He gave up all, and after some time at the missionary training-school, went out, as will be seen by the following narrative, to win whole tribes to the Lord Jesus. Upon his arrival at Fort Simpson, he says, "I found located here nine tribes of Tsimpsean Indians, numbering by actual count 2300 souls. To attempt to describe their condition would be but to produce a dark and revolting picture of human depravity. The dark mantle of degrading superstition enveloped them all, and their savage spirits, swayed by pride, jealousy, and revenge, were ever hurrying them on to deeds of blood. Their history was little else than a chapter of crime and misery. But worse was to come. The following year the discovery of gold brought in a rush of miners. Fire-water now began its reign of terror, and debauchery its work of desolation. On every hand were raving drunkards and groaning victims. The medicine-man's rattle and the voice of wailing seldom ceased."

Some of these scenes are thus depicted by Mr. Dunçan :

"The other day we were called upon to witness a terrible scene. An old chief in cold blood ordered a slave to be dragged to the beach, murdered, and thrown into the water. His orders were quickly obeyed. The victim was a poor woman. Two or three reasons are assigned for this foul act. One is that it is to take away the disgrace attached to his daughter, who had been suffering for some time with a ball wound in the arm. Another report is that he does not expect his daughter to recover, so he has killed this slave in order that she may prepare for the coming of his daughter into the unseen world. I did not see the murder, but immediately after saw crowds of people running out of the houses near to where the corpse was thrown and forming themselves into groups at a good distance away, from fear of what was to follow. Presently two bands of furious wretches appeared, each headed by a man in a state of nudity. They gave vent to the most unearthly sounds, and the naked men made themselves look as unearthly as possible, proceeding in a creeping kind of stoop, and stepping like two proud horses, at the same time shooting forward each arm alternately, which they held out at full length for a little time in the most defiant manner. Besides this, the continual jerking of their heads back, causing their long black hair to twist about, added much to their savage appearance. For some time they pretended to be seeking for the body, and the instant they came where it lay they commenced screaming and rushing around it like so many angry wolves. Finally they seized it, dragged it out of the water, and laid it on the beach, where they commenced tearing it to pieces with their teeth. The two bands of men immediately surrounded them, and so hid their horrid work. In a few minutes the crowd broke again, when each of the naked cannibals appeared with half of

DOG-EATERS.

the body in his hands. Separating a few yards, they commenced, amid horrid yells, their still more horrid feast of eating the raw dead body. The two bands of men belonged to that class called 'medicine-men.'

"I may mention that each party has some characteristics peculiar to itself; but in a more general sense their divisions are but three, viz., those who eat human bodies, the dog-eaters, and those who have no custom of the kind. Early in the morning the pupils would be out on the beach, or on the rocks, in a state of nudity. Each had a place in the front of his own tribe; nor did intense cold interfere in the slightest degree. After the poor creature had crept about, jerking his head and screaming for some time, a party of men would rush out, and after surrounding him would commence singing. The dog-eating party occasionally carried a dead dog to their pupil, who forthwith commenced to tear it in the most dog-like manner. The party of attendants kept up a low growling noise, or a whoop, which was seconded by a screeching noise made from an instrument, which they believe to be the abode of a spirit. In a little time the naked youth would start up again and proceed a few more yards in a crouching posture, with his arms pushed out behind him, and tossing his flowing black hair. All the while he is earnestly watched by the group about him, and when he pleases to sit down they again surround him and commence singing. This kind of thing goes on, with several different additions, for some time. Before the prodigy finally retires he takes a run into every house belonging to his tribe, and is followed by his train. When this is done, in some cases he has a ramble on the tops of the same houses, during which he is anxiously watched by his attendants, as if they expected his flight. By and by he condescends to come down, and they then follow him to his den, which is marked by a rope made of red bark, being hung over the doorway so as to prevent any person from ignorantly violating its precincts. None are allowed to enter that house but those connected with the art ; all I know, therefore, of their further proceedings is that they keep up a furious hammering, singing, and screeching for hours during the day.

" Of all these parties, none are so much dreaded as the cannibals. One morning I was called to witness a stir in the camp which had been caused by this set. When I reached the gallery I saw hundreds of Tsimpseans sitting in their canoes, which they had just pushed away from the beach. I was told that the cannibal party were in search of a body to devour, and if they failed to find a dead one, it was probable they would seize the first living one that came in their way ; so that all the people living near the cannibals' house had taken to their canoes to escape being torn to pieces. It is the custom among these Indians to burn their dead ; but I suppose for these occasions they take care to deposit a corpse somewhere in order to satisfy these inhuman wretches.

" These, then, are some of the things and scenes which occur in the day during the winter months, while the nights are taken up with amusements,

SCHOOL OPENED. 281

singing and dancing. Occasionally the medicine parties invite people to their several houses, and exhibit tricks before them of various kinds. Some of the actors appear as bears, while others wear masks, the parts of which are moved by strings. The great feature of their proceedings is to pretend to murder and then to restore to life. The cannibal, on such occasions, is generally supplied with two, three, or four human bodies, which he tears to pieces before his audience. Several persons, either from bravado or as a charm, present their arms for him to bite. I have seen several whom he had thus bitten, and I hear two have died from the effects."

Sustained by the Divine Arm, Mr. Duncan set himself resolutely to work. Unforeseen difficulties met him at every turn. But he persevered. At length the Gospel leaven began to work. One after another began to listen and forsake their heathen practices until quite a body of converts gathered around him.

On June 28th, 1858, he opened the first school in the house of a chief, with twenty six children and fifteen adults. The interest grew so rapidly that in July the erection of a school building was commenced. Before the close of the year there were one hundred and forty children and fifty adults in attendance.

On the 20th of December a chief named Legaic, accompanied by a party of medicine-men, enraged because the people were losing their interest in sorcery through Mr. Duncan's teachings, attempted to murder him.

This same Legaic became afterward an earnest

Christian, and, like Saul, was very zealous for the faith he had once sought to destroy. Upon one occasion, in reply to an old man who had said that if Mr. Duncan had come when the first white traders came, the Tsimpseans had long since been good ; but they had been allowed to grow up in sin ; they had seen nothing among the first whites who came among them to unsettle them in their old habits ; that these had rather added to them fresh sins, and now their sins were so deep laid they (he and the other old people) could not change, Legaic said, " I am a chief, a Tsimpsean chief. You know I have been bad, very bad, as bad as any one here. I have grown up, and grown old in sin, but God has changed my heart, and he can change yours. Think not to excuse yourselves in your sin by saying you are too old and too bad to mend. Nothing is impossible with God. Come to God ; try his way ; he can save you."

In April, 1860, Mr. Duncan visited the settlements on the Naas River, where he received a warm welcome. One of the chiefs, rising in the council and spreading his hands toward heaven, said, " Pity us, Great Spirit in heaven, pity us. This chief (pointing to Mr. Duncan) has come to tell us about thee. It is good, Great Spirit. We want to hear. Who ever came to tell our forefathers thy will ? No ! no ! But this chief has pitied us and come. He has thy book. We will hear. We will receive thy word. We will obey."

At the close of one of Mr. Duncan's addresses the people responded, " Good is your speech. Good,

TRADITION CONCERNING THE WHITES. 283

good, good news. We greatly desire to learn the book. We wish our children to learn." After which one of the chiefs arose and addressed the people as follows : " We are not to call upon stones and stars now, but Jesus. Jesus will hear. Jesus is our Saviour. Jesus ! Jesus ! Jesus ! Jesus Christ ! Good news, good news ! Listen all. Put away your sins. God has sent his word. Jesus is our Saviour. Take away my sins, Jesus. Make me good, Jesus."

In May Mr. Duncan visited the site of a deserted village, which was afterward chosen as the site of the Christian village of Metlahkatlah.

Encamping near an adjacent village, an old chief gave him the following tradition of the first appearance of the whites :

" A large canoe of Indians were busy catching halibut in one of these channels. A thick mist enveloped them. Suddenly they heard a noise as if a large animal was striking through the water. Immediately they concluded that a monster from the deep was in pursuit of them. With all speed they hauled up their fishing-lines, seized the paddles, and strained every nerve to reach the shore. Still the plunging noise came nearer. Every minute they expected to be engulfed within the jaws of some huge creature. However, they reached the land, jumped on shore, and turned round in breathless anxiety to watch the approach of the monster. Soon a boat, filled with strange-looking men, emerged from the mist. The pulling of the oars had caused the strange noise. Though somewhat relieved of fear, the Indians stood spell-bound with amazement. The strangers landed, and beckoned the Indians to come to them and bring them some fish. One of them had over his shoulder what was supposed only to be a stick : presently he pointed it to a bird that was flying past ; a violent poo went forth ; down came the bird to the ground. The Indians died. As they reviv' .. again they questioned each other as to their state, whether any were dead, and what each had felt. The whites then made signs for a fire to be lighted. The Indians proceeded at once, according to their usual tedious fashion of rubbing two sticks together. The strangers laughed; and one of them, snatching up a handful of dry grass, struck a spark into a little powder placed under it. Instantly flashed another poo and a blaze. The Indians died. After this the newcomers wanted some fish boiling. The Indians therefore put the fish and water into one of their square wooden buckets, and set some stones in the fire, intending, when they were hot, to cast them into the vessel, and thus boil the food. The whites were not satisfied with this way. One of them fetched a tin kettle out of the boat, put the fish and the water into it, and then, strange to say, set it on the fire. The Indians looked on with astonishment. However, the kettle did not consume, the water did not run into the fire. Then again the Indians died. When the fish was eaten the strangers put a kettle of rice on the fire. The Indians looked at each other and whispered, 'Akshahn, akshahn ' (maggots, maggots). The rice being cooked, some molasses was mixed with it. The Indians stared and said, ' Coutzee um tsakah ahket ' (the grease of dead peo-

KINDLING A FIRE BY FRICTION.

ple). The whites then offered this to the Indians, who refused with disgust. Seeing this the whites sat down and eat it themselves. The sight stunned the Indians, and again they all died. Some other similar wonders were worked, and the amazement which the Indians felt each time they termed death. The Indians' turn had now come to make the white strangers die. They dressed their heads and painted their faces. A nok-nok (wonder-working spirit) possessed them. They came slowly and solemnly, seated themselves before the whites, then suddenly lifted up their heads and stared. Their reddened eyes had the desired effect. The whites died."

That same season, at the request of the Government, Mr. Duncan visited the large number of Indians congregated at Victoria. While there, Shooquanahts, one of his school-boys, aged about fourteen, made the following records in his writing-book :

"April 10.—I could not sleep last night. I must work hard last night. I could not be lazy last night. No good lazy—very bad. We must learn to make all things. When we understand reading and writing, then it will very easy. Perhaps two grass, then we understand. If we no understand to read and to write, then he will very angry Mr. Duncan. If we understand about good people, then we will very happy."

"April 17 : School, Fort Simpson.—Shooquanahts not two hearts—always one my heart. Some boys always two hearts Only one Shooquanahts— not two heart, no. If I steal anything then God will see. Bad people no care about Son of God when will come troubled hearts, foolish people. Then he will very much cry. What good cry? Nothing. No care about our Saviour; always forget. By and by will understand about the Son of God."

" May 17.—I do not understand some prayers— only few prayers I understand; not all I understand, no. I wish to understand all prayers. When I understand all prayers, then I always prayer our Saviour Jesus Christ. I want to learn to prayer to Jesus Christ our Saviour: by and by I understand all about our Saviour Christ; when I understand all about our Saviour, then I will happy when I die. If I do not learn about our Saviour Jesus, then I will very troubled my heart when I die. It is good for us when we learn about our Saviour Jesus. When I understand about our Saviour Jesus, then I will very happy when I die. '

As the number of converts increased, Mr. Duncan felt more and more the necessity of establishing a new village where the Christian Indians could be separated from the sights and influences of heathenism. As early as May, 1859, the matter had been considered, but it was not until May, 1862, that the change was made. At that time he removed the mission premises, and was accompanied by fifty faithful ones some twenty miles down the coast to a new place, which they named Metlahkatlah. At this point they established a Christian village, with the following regulations:

'1. To give up their 'Ahlied,' or Indian devilry; 2. To cease calling in conjurors when sick; 3. To cease gambling ; 4. To cease giving away their property for display ; 5. To cease painting their faces ; 6. To cease drinking intoxicating drink ; 7. To rest on the Sabbath ; 8. To attend religious instruction ; 9. To send their children to school ; 10. To be cleanly ; 11. To be industrious ; 12. To be peaceful ; 13 To be liberal and honest in trade ; 14. To build neat houses ; 15. To pay the village tax."

The removal, on the 27th of May, was a very solemn occasion. Mr. Duncan says :

"The Indians came out of their lodges and sat round in a semicircle, watching the proceedings. They knew something was going to happen, but they did not know what. When an Indian watches, he sits upon the ground, brings his knees up to his chin, wraps his mantle round him, puts his head down, and, mute and motionless, looks at a distance like a stone. Thus they were seated, and the question was, 'Will any one stand out in the midst of the scoffing heathen and declare themselves Christians?' First there came two or three, trembling, and said they were willing to go anywhere, and to give up all for the blessed Saviour's sake. Others were then encouraged ; and that day fifty stood forth, and gathered together such things as they needed, put them into their canoes, and away they went. On that day every tie was broken ; children were separated from their parents, husbands from wives, brothers from sisters ; houses, land, and all things were left—such was the power at work in their minds. All that were ready to go with me occupied six canoes, and we numbered about fifty souls—men, women, and children. Many Indians were seated on the beach watching our departure with solemn and anxious faces, and some promised to follow us in a few days. The party with me seemed filled with solemn joy as we pushed off, feeling that their long-looked-for flit had actually commenced. I felt we were beginning an eventful page in the history of this poor people, and earnestly sighed to God for his help and blessing. The next day, the 28th of May, we arrived at our new home about two P.M. The Indians I had sent on before with the raft I found hard at work, clearing ground and sawing plank. They had carried all the raft up from the beach, excepting a few heavy beams, erected two temporary houses, and had planted about four bushels of potatoes for me. Every night we assembled, a happy family, for singing and prayer. I gave an address on each occasion from some portion of scriptural truth suggested to me by the events of the day.

"On the 6th of June a fleet of about thirty canoes arrived from Fort Simpson. They formed nearly the whole of one tribe, called Keetlahn, with two of their chiefs. We now numbered between three hundred and four hundred souls, and our evening meetings became truly delightful."

In April, 1863, the Bishop of British Columbia visited the new station and baptized fifty-seven adults and children. He writes: "It was my office to examine the candidates for baptism. I was several days engaged in the work. One day I was engaged from eight o'clock in the morning until one o'clock at night. It was the last day I had, and they pressed

AN INDIAN FAMILY ON THE YUKON RIVER.

on me continually to be examined. Night and darkness came. The Indians usually go to bed with the sun, but now they turned night into day, in order that they might be 'fixed in God's ways,' they said. 'Any more Indians?' I kept saying, as eight o'clock, nine o'clock, ten o'clock, twelve o'clock, and one o'clock came, and there were always more Indians wishing to be 'fixed' on God's side. I shall never forget the scene. The little oil-lamp was not enough to dispel the gloom or darkness of the room, but its light was sufficient to cast a reflection on the countenance of each Indian as he or she sat before me. The Indian countenance is usually inexpressive of emotion, but now, when they spoke of prayer and trust in God, there was the uplifted eye and evident fervor; and when they spoke of their sins there was a downcast look, the flush came and went on their cheeks, and the big tear frequently coursed from their manly eyes. Their whole hearts seemed to speak out in their countenances."

One day an Indian from a distance came to Mr. Duncan, saying, "The Indians tell me that you have a book which the Great Spirit wrote, and it tells about me; is that true?" Being assured that it was, he added, "Can I see it?" Mr. Duncan stepped into his private room and brought out a large Bible, which he opened before the man. The Indian, gazing at it intently, said, "Do you say the Great Spirit wrote that?" Being answered in the affirmative, he continued, "Then tell me what is in it. Oh, tell me quick! I want to know what the Great Spirit says to me. I want to do what the Great Spirit says."

The new settlement has now grown to one thousand people, forming the healthiest and strongest settlement on the coast. "Rules have been laid down for the regulation of the community, to which all residents are obliged to conform, and the use of spirituous liquors strictly prohibited. All are required to keep the Sabbath, attend church, and send their children to school. Industrious habits are diligently encouraged, and the people educated as farmers, blacksmiths, carpenters, merchants, etc. They live in well-built cottages, and have a beautiful Gothic church capable of seating one thousand persons. It is modelled after the old English cathedral, and was built by the Indian mechanics of that village. The average winter attendance is six hundred to eight hundred. They have also a school building that will accommodate seven hundred pupils. Besides these they have carpenter and blacksmith shops, storehouse, saw-mill, etc., all owned and managed by the Indians ; while all around the bay are well cultivated gardens and potato patches. The main street of the village along the beach is lighted with street lamps. Five hundred and seventy-nine adults have been baptized at this mission ; four hundred and ten infant baptisms ; two hundred and forty-three deaths among the Christian portion of the people ; one hundred and thirty-seven Christian marriages, independent of those who were found married according to their tribal customs. A large number of catechumens are under instruction as candidates for church-membership.

The population of 1000 is divided into ten companies or wards, each having its elder to look after its religious services, its chief as leader in social gatherings, and one or two constables. The village has a brass band of twenty-four instruments, a public reading-room and public guest-house for the lodging of strange Indians. Fifty two-story dwelling-houses were in process of erection at the time of my visit. The present mission force is Mr. William Duncan, superintendent, Rev. W. H. Collison and wife, and David Leask, native assistant.

These Indians are a happy, industrious, prosperous community of former savages and cannibals, saved by the grace of God. This is the oldest and most successful Indian mission on that coast, and illustrates what one consecrated man by the Divine help can accomplish.

In 1864 a new mission was established at Kincolith, for the five tribes of Tsimpseans on the Nasse River, by Rev. R. A. Doolan. He was succeeded by Rev. Robert Tomlinson, M.D., who remained until 1879, when Mr. Tomlinson left to establish a new mission. The village is now in charge of Mr. Henry Schutt, teacher. This mission was established upon the same plan as Metlahkatlah, and numbers about one hundred and fifty people. About forty miles above Kincolith, on the Nasse River, a new mission has been established at Kittackdamin, and placed in charge of Arthur, a Nishkah Indian catechist. A school-house has been erected and a good school started.

Another native teacher has been placed at Kitwingach, on the Skeena River, one hundred miles from Kittackdamin,

On November 1st, 1876, Rev. W. II. Collison, of Metlahkatlah, established a mission at Massett, on Queen Charlotte's Island, among the Hydahs. These are the most daring and blood-thirsty tribe on the Pacific coast, and in days past have not hesitated to attack and capture European ships. He had previously visited them in July. A large Indian dance-house was secured and fitted up for a mission. A morning school for women and children and an evening one for men were opened. Feeling deeply the need for it, he also opened a home for girls. During the past season the average attendance at the morning school was about fifty. At the Sabbath services the attendance was from three hundred to four hundred. The work has been greatly prospered. Thirty catechumens are under instruction as candidates for church-membership, among whom are four principal chiefs. One of the chiefs, Cow-hoe, is under special instruction for a teacher.

Last spring the work at Metlahkatlah requiring Mr. Collison's presence, he returned with his excellent wife to that station. And the Rev. George Sneath was sent out from England to take his place at Massett. Mr. Sneath was originally sent out to the Central African mission, but his health failed, and he was transferred to the north-west coast. Before leaving, Mr. Collison wrote from Massett:

"One of the principal chiefs died a short time since. I visited him during his illness, and held service in his house weekly for the five weeks preceding his death. On the morning of the day on which he died I visited him, and found him surrounded by

DEATH OF A CHIEF. 297

the men of his tribe and the principal medicine-man, who kept up his incantations and charms to the last. He was sitting up, and appeared glad to see me, and in answer to my inquiries he informed me that he was very low indeed and his heart weak. I directed him to withdraw his mind from everything, and look only to Jesus, who alone could help him. He thanked me again and again while I instructed him ; and when I asked him if he would like me to pray with him, he replied that he would, very much. I then called upon all to kneel, and, with bowed head, he followed my petitions earnestly. He informed me that, had he been spared, he would have been one of the first in the way of God ; but I endeavored to show him that even then he might be so by faith in the Lord Jesus Christ.

"His death was announced by the firing of several cannon which they have in the village. On my entering the house the scene which presented itself was indescribable—shrieking, dancing, tearing and burning their hair in the fire ; while the father of the deceased, who had just been pulled out of the fire, rushed to it again and threw himself upon it. He was with difficulty removed, and I directed two men to hold him while I endeavored to calm the tumult.

"I was very much shocked to find that a young man—a slave—had been accused by the medicine-men as having bewitched the chief and induced his sickness. In consequence of this he had been stripped and bound hand and foot in an old out-house, and thus kept for some days without food. I only learned this about one hour before the death of the chief, and it was well I heard it even then, as I learned that they had determined to shoot him, and a man had been told of who had his gun ready for the purpose. I lost no time in calling the chiefs and the friends of the deceased, and showed them the wickedness and sinfulness of such proceedings, and how by their thus acting they had probably kept up a feeling of revenge in the mind of their friend who had just expired. They accepted my advice and had him unbound, and he came to the mission-house to have his wounds dressed. His wrists were swollen to an immense size, and his back, from hip to shoulder, lacerated and burned to the bone by torches of pitch-pine. He was deeply grateful to me for having saved him.

" The dead chief was laid out, and all those of his crest came from the opposite village, bringing a large quantity of swan's-down, which they scattered over and around the corpse. At my suggestion they departed from the usual custom of dressing and painting the dead, and instead of placing the corpse in a sitting posture they consented to place it on the back. The remains were decently interred, and I gave an address and prayed; thus their custom of placing the dead in hollowed poles, carved and erected near the house, has been broken through, and since this occurred many of the remains which were thus placed have been buried.

" Dancing, which was carried on every night without intermission during our first winter on the islands, has been greatly checked. Several, including two of the chiefs, have given it up entirely. The medicine-men have informed them that those who give up dancing will die soon. They are well aware that the abandonment of this practice will weaken their influence, and hence their opposition."

Some three or four years ago the head chief of the Indians upon the northern end of Vancouver's Island, at Fort Rupert, visited Metlahaktlah, and asked for a teacher, saying that "a rope had been thrown out from Metlahpatlah which was encircling and drawing together all the Indian tribes into one common brotherhood."

In response to his earnest entreaty, it was at length arranged that Rev. A. J. Hall should go and establish a mission among them. This he did, opening a school on April 1st, 1878. The tribe number about 3500, a strong and intelligent race, given to deadly feuds, cannibal feasts, slave-catching expeditions, and infanticide.

The Roman Catholics have had no less than twelve priests among these people at different times, but all have left without accomplishing anything.

Mr. Hall has an attendance of from forty to sixty at the day-school, and frequently audiences of a hundred upon the Sabbath.

In a late letter he says : " The medicine-men still exercise much power. A few days since I went to see a sick woman. I entered the house and heard strange noises. A medicine-woman, with her back turned to me, was blowing very scientifically on the breast of the sick woman, and occasionally making a peculiar howl. I watched the practitioner unobserved, and when she turned round and saw me she gave me a grin of recognition and then continued her blowing. For this she was paid two blankets. A famous doctor was recently sent for from a neighboring village. I heard him blowing in the same way, and for his visit he received thirty blankets. These people are divided into 'clans,' and each clan imitates an animal when dancing. The children follow their fathers and grandfathers in the same dance year by year. One party, when they perform, are hung up with hooks in a triangular frame, one hook being stuck into the back and two more into the legs, and suspended in this way they are carried through the village. Another clan have large fish-hooks put into their flesh, to which lines are attached. The victim struggles to get away, and those who hold the lines haul him back ; eventually his flesh is torn and he escapes. By suffering in this way they keep up the dignity of their ancestors, and are renowned for their bravery."

During Mr. Tomlinson's residence at Kincolith he was accustomed to make an annual visit to the Indians in the Kish-pi-youx valley, on the Upper Skeena. Upon the recommendation of Bishop Bomas, Mr. Tomlinson removed there last April and opened up a mission farm, from which he hopes to reach several tribes. Having long treated their sick at the mission hospital at Kincolith, he is said to have acquired great influence over them.

The Church Missionary Society are so much encouraged by the progress of the missions on the North Pacific coast that they have erected them into a bishopric, called Caledonia, and appointed

Rev. W. Ridley as bishop. For the more efficient working of his field he has received funds to purchase a small mission steamer, which is very essential for carrying on the work among the many islands of his diocese.

The success which has attended the labors of these British missionaries should be a great encouragement to the American church in her work among the neighboring tribes of Alaska.

After a pleasant visit at Metlahkatlah, I returned by canoe to Fort Simpson,

A CANOE VOYAGE.

CHAPTER XI.

Missions of the Methodist Church of Canada in British Columbia
—A Great Revival—Wonderful Experiences.

> " The light shall glance on distant lands,
> And Indian tribes, in joyful bands,
> Come with exulting haste to prove
> The power and greatness of His love."

THE missions to the Indians on the north-west coast of America have called out three remarkable men —the Rev. Innocentius Veniaminoff, of the Greek Church, who, commencing as an humble priest in Alaska, was made bishop and then primate of the Greek Church of all Russia ; Mr. William Duncan, of the Church Missionary Society of London, who built up the model Indian village of Metlahkatlah, and the Rev. Thomas Crosby, missionary of the Methodist Church of Canada at Fort Simpson, on the edge of Alaska. On the 28th day of February, 1862, a local preacher in the Methodist Church, Mr. Crosby left Canada for Indian work in British Columbia.

In the spring of 1863 he commenced teaching an Indian mission school at Nanaimo. In six months he so far secured a knowledge of the language that he could preach in it. In 1867 he became a candidate for ordination, and took a circuit extending up and

A GREAT MEDICINE MAN.

down the coast among the Indians for one hundred and eighty miles, and up the Fraser River to Yale. In 1869 his first field was visited by an extensive revival, and hundreds among the Flathead Indians were brought to Christ. His great success attracted the attention of his denomination, so that when a picked man was wanted to go to the tribes in the distant north he was selected. The work among those tribes had commenced in a remarkable manner.

In 1862 there was in Victoria a Mrs. Dix, who was a full-blooded Indian woman, the daughter of a great chief, and a chiefess in her own right. When a child she was at stated times taken up a great river in a canoe and taught to worship a large mountain-peak. Her mother's god was a fish. Desiring to learn something of the white man's God, she commenced attending religious services in Victoria, and followed it up for seven years without finding light or comfort. About 1868 a great medicine-man named "Amos," who in his incantations had torn in pieces with his teeth and eaten dead bodies, commenced attending the Methodist Church and prayer-meeting. This called the attention of the church to the condition of the Indian population, and a Sabbath-school was started for their benefit. The second Sabbath no Indian was present at the school. Upon visiting their camp they were found making a medicine-man, with all the accompanying cruelties. But the school was persevered in. Amos was one of the first converts, and became a class-leader. About this time Mrs. Dix found her way to the school and to Christ. A revival commenced among the Indians, during which meetings were kept up for nine weeks, and numbers were brought into the church.

With her own conversion Mrs. Dix became anxious for the conversion of her daughter-in-law and son, Alfred, who was chief of a tribe several hundred miles up the coast. She spent whole nights in prayer that God would bring him to Victoria under the revival influences. She asked her friends, white and Indian, to join her in this petition. During the meetings that son, who had not been home for years, landed from the steamer at Victoria, after a canoe-load of whiskey. He was prevailed on to attend church with his wife and mother. All the depravity of his nature rose up against what he had heard and seen. He was angry at his mother, himself, and everybody. Still more earnest prayer was then made for him, and prayer prevailed. Both he and his wife were brought to Christ. With the fire kindled in their own hearts, they hastened back to their own people, near the Alaska line, bearing the glad tidings of great joy. As of old when Parthians and Medes and dwellers in Asia and strangers at Rome and others carried back to their own people the fire and tidings of the pentecostal season, so these Indians carried the power of the Gospel with them to their homes at the Skeena, the Nasse, the Tastazellaroka, and other places too numerous to mention.

An old gray-haired, blind Indian, hundreds of miles away, heard the good news that Jesus Christ came into the world to save sinners---that he who made the sun and moon, the mountains and rivers and fish, had sent his boy to the world to take the "bad out

THE BLIND INDIAN. 307

of him." How his heart leaped for joy ! Again and again he had gone into the deep, gloomy cañons of the mountains and fasted by the day and the week to get the bad out of him. Under the lashings of conscience he had gone to the medicine-men of his people and laid piles of costly furs before them, if they would only bring him peace. As gray hairs came, and he himself became a medicine-man, in his desperation he had, after the horrible rites of his order, torn the flesh from half-putrid human corpses to get the bad out of him, but all in vain. And now he hears of one who can certainly take the bad out of him. He wants to go to him at once. He wants to hear all about him. His Indian informer can only assure him that Jesus is the Saviour, and that if he could go to the coast there is a man there that would tell him all about Jesus. Taking a grandson to lead him, he starts for the coast.

Many a lonely mile they paddled their canoe, and many the suns that set upon their wild evening camp. When near the coast they were met by a Christian. The blind man was ever repeating to himself, as he groped along, " Jesus Christ came into the world to save sinners." This attracted the attention of the Christian, who halted the party and learned the above history. The Indian was directed to a mission station, and, like the Ethiopian eunuch of old, went on his way rejoicing.

Alfred, the chief, upon his return from Victoria, commenced at once to hold meetings among his own people at Fort Simpson. In connection with his wife he opened a day-school, which was soon attended by over two hundred pupils. Letter after letter was sent to Victoria urging the appointment of a missionary.

In the spring of 1874 they were visited by Rev. W. Pollard, of Victoria, who held meetings among them and baptized a large number. After the departure of Mr. Pollard the meetings were carried on by the people themselves and with the aid of the Holy Spirit. So that when Rev. Thomas Crosby reached Fort Simpson, in the fall of 1874, he found a glorious work of grace in progress, and not a single family that had not already renounced paganism and were impatiently awaiting his arrival to be taught more perfectly in the new way

It is proper to say that this preparatory work was partly due to the leaven of Mr. Duncan's labors for the Church Missionary Society and partly to the revival at Victoria.

With enthusiasm Mr. and Mrs. Crosby set themselves to the work, and by God's blessing a village of Christian Indians has grown up around them. Their beautiful new church is Gothic in style, fifty by eighty feet in size, with buttresses, and a tower one hundred and forty feet high.

During the finishing of the church an unusual storm unroofed it, and for a time the whole church was in danger of being destroyed. As the first portion of the roof came down with a crash, an old Indian ran to one of the stores, and securing a coil of rope ran back to the church out of breath. Younger and stronger men mounted the swaying building and fastened the rope to the gable end. Others

METHODIST CHURCH AND PARSONAGE, FORT SIMPSON, B. C.

tightened the rope and fastened the other end to a large stump. Then kneeling down around the stump in a beating storm they uncovered their heads, and one prayed that the Lord would have pity upon them and spare his house, saying, "Lord, you have taken the roof off your house; that is enough. Now, Lord, don't do any more." The walls of the building being firmly lashed with ropes to neighboring rocks and stumps, the people repaired to the schoolhouse. A chief arose and called out that it was not a time for long speeches, but action. Instantly twenty or thirty men left the house, and the missionary was alarmed lest they were offended; others followed them, but soon they commenced returning with rolls of blankets (the currency of that region) on their shoulders and laid them in front of the teacher's desk, as their offering to the Lord. The fire was kindled, and amid tears and laughter, blankets, coats, shirts, shawls, guns, finger and ear rings, bracelets, furs, and indeed almost everything that could be turned into money, were laid upon the table of offering, to the value of $400—a striking commentary on the constraining love of Christ in their hearts.

Schools of various kinds have been successfully established. The day-school in winter numbers about one hundred and twenty. The Sunday-school is divided into three parts—before morning service Bible-classes are held, when the previous Sunday lesson is taken up, read, and discussed. In the afternoon the children are taken to the school-house, where lessons suitable to their understanding are given by Mrs. Crosby and Miss C. S. Knott. Mr. Crosby has the adults under his care at the same time in the church.

Thus the whole church is reached, and a whole tribe are moving steadily forward to a higher civilization. Under the influence of Christianity the Indians are abandoning their large houses, which are the common abode of several families, and building separate houses for each family. During the past two years sixty such dwellings have been erected by Indian mechanics, and the old houses are fast disappearing with other remnants of their old civilization.

Under the leadership of Mr. Crosby the Indians have an annual industrial fair, at which small premiums are given for the best specimens of carving in wood or silver, models of dwellings and canoes, best vegetables, best kept garden, best made window-sash, panelled doors, cured salmon, etc:

During the winter of '77 and '78 a revival came with great power among them. One evening a great crowd came and asked to be admitted to the church. As Rev. Mr. Crosby was absent, his able and efficient assistant, Miss C. S. Knott, went into the church with them. The whole assembly seemed moved to strong crying and tears and excited confessions of sin. After a lengthy meeting she dismissed them and closed the church, but they refused to go home. They gathered in groups in the churchyard, although it was raining almost incessantly. They scarcely eat or slept, neglected themselves and their children. The whole place was one of weeping. These strong manifestations lasted three days and nights, when they calmed down.

HEATHEN DANCE, ALASKA.

Mr. Crosby returning, meetings were held for a number of weeks, until large numbers were brought into the church. Many flocked in from the neighboring tribes, and, finding Jesus, returned to their own people to spread the story of salvation.

As at Fort Simpson, so on the Naas River the converted natives from Fort Simpson carried the messages of salvation into the regions beyond in advance of the white missionary. And upon the shores of the Naas, where for ages had been heard the rattle and wild howling of incantations of medicine-men, was heard for the first time the song of redeeming love. Mr. Crosby made several trips to the Naas villages.

In response to their earnest entreaties he secured the appointment of Rev. Alfred E. Greene. Mr. Greene, accompanied by Mr. Crosby, reached the lower Naas Indian village August 9th, 1877, and met a very warm welcome. Guns were fired, flags hoisted on trees and poles, and the population turned out *en masse*, and many rejoiced that the day was breaking on the Naas people after a long dark night.

A chief who was at Naas, and whose adopted daughter is a member of the church, said, " I heard my daughter sing and read and pray. I want all this people to do the same. *Give us this great light.* We have heard of the Fort Simpson people, how wise they are. They used to come up here to fight us, but they don't any more ; all peace now. We want to be just like them."

One old chief, as he leaned upon his staff, said, " I am getting old ; my body is getting weaker every day ; I am obliged to have three legs to walk with now (referring to his staff) ; this tells me I shall soon die. I don't know what hour I shall be called away ; I want to hear about the great God, and I want my children to be taught to read the Good Book ; I want them to go in the new way ; we are tired of the old fashion."

Another said, " My heart got very warm last night when I heard God's Word. I heard a little last spring. I was down the river and saw Mr. Crosby, and I took just a little of the good medicine, and my heart felt well, but after the missionary went away I had trouble, and my heart got all mixed up. I did bad and my heart got very sick, so I say to myself, When the good medicine comes again I will take more of it. Last night I took more of it ; now my eyes open and everything look beautiful." Then as he pointed up the river he added, " There are ten tribes of people living up there, missionary ; we give them all to you. Go and see them ; they all want to know the Great Spirit." They then presented them the following touching address :

" We, the chiefs and people of the Naas, welcome you from our hearts on your safe arrival here to begin in earnest the mission work you promised us last spring.

" Our past life has been bad—*very bad*. We have been so long left in darkness that we fear you will not be able to do much for our old people, but for our young we have great hopes. We wish from our hearts to have our young men, women, and children read and write, so that they may understand the duties they owe to their great Creator and to each other.

"You will find great difficulties in the way of such work, but great changes cannot be expected in one day. You must not get discouraged by a little trouble, and we tell you again that we will all help you as much as we can.

"We believe this work to be of God. We have prayed, as you told us, and now we think that God has heard our prayers and sent you to us, and it seems to us like the day breaking in on our darkness, and we think that before long the great Sun will shine upon us and give us more light.

"We hope to see the white men that settle among us set us a good example, as they have had the light so long they know what is right and what is wrong. We hope they will assist us to do what is good, that we may become better and better every day by following their example.

"We again welcome you from our hearts, and hope that the mission here will be like a great rock, never to be moved or washed away; and in order to this we will pray to the Great Spirit that his blessing may rest upon this mission and upon us all.

(Signed) "CHIEF OF THE MOUNTAINS,
"And six other chiefs."

Messrs. Crosby and Greene commenced a series of meetings extending over five days. Three services were held each day. Soon the house was filled with the cries of Indians under conviction of sin. These services were continued for weeks by Mr. Greene. God's spirit was present with a power that shook the heathenism of that section to its foundation. Desperate and depraved sorcerers bowed at the foot of the cross and were made new creatures in Christ Jesus.

An instance of this is thus given by the missionary: "A chief of considerable influence, who has been bitter against any missionary coming here, came to me to tell how miserable he had been for two weeks. He said, 'God had troubled his heart because he was so wicked, and he was determined he would not be a Christian, but he had no rest day or night, and he was angry with everybody; he got so bad that his wife could not live with him any longer.' Then he said when we talked to him in his house, he saw it was all sin that made this trouble, and something told him to leave his sins and become a Christian, but then he thought of his blankets that he potlatched* last year, and as he gave away all he had, next year he would commence to serve God and receive it back, so that he thought he would not get a new heart till he got his property back. 'But,' said he, 'my heart got so sick I could neither eat or work or sleep; I was nearly dead; then I think of God, and Sunday, while in the house, as I hear God's word, I say I will give my heart, blankets, and all to God, and the same moment all

---

* Potlatch means a gift. It is a custom of the northern tribes for one who aspires to the chieftainship to make a great feast and give away the accumulation of years, with the expectation of receiving it all back with interest in the future.

my trouble went away—my heart became so happy sometimes I think I am not the same man.' He went and told his wife ; they became reconciled, and as he told his experience in the crowded class-meeting, many wept for joy.

"He put his idols away, he buried his bad medicines in a quaking bog, he married his aged consort, the companion of his life, and hand in hand with her he approached the table of the Lord. Night after night he comes to learn from the missionary's lips the sweetly simple yet expressive prayer of Christ, ' Our Father which art in heaven, hallowed be thy name.' "

As the result of these meetings a class of seventy-five was at once formed.

The following winter an old man, who had opposed the coming of the missionary, as he felt death approaching requested his children to bring him to the mission. He was very anxious for the missionary to be with him. He spent much of the time in prayer. Several times he asked for a Bible ; Mr. Greene sent him one. The day before he died the missionary saw the Bible tied to the top of a stick about three feet long, which was set in the ground near his head. He asked, " Why do you tie the book there ?" The old man answered, " I can't read, but I know that is the great Word, so when my heart gets weak I just look up at the book and say, Father, that is your book ; no one to teach me to read ; very good you help me ; then my heart gets stronger, the bad goes away." He told his friends not to bury him the old heathen way, but to let the missionary bury him, and the next morning calmly passed away, trusting in Jesus.

A small residence was erected for the missionary, and a school-house and chapel, thirty by forty feet in size. Getting started in the lower village, another mission was established in the upper one, twenty-five miles distant. This is the darkest and most wicked village on the river. They do not bury their dead, but have a feast, make a great fire in the house, throw on the body, and dance around it while it burns ; but they are seeking for light. Heathenism was carried on by doctors and conjurors to a great degree, ten being at work when the missionaries arrived. They preached the first night to a large congregation. The next day they visited the sick, giving them medicine and pointing them to Jesus. A large number of the people followed them from house to house, eager to catch every word. On Sunday the large house was filled ; many, being unable to get even standing room, climbed up the roof to the open square, through which the smoke escapes, and there listened attentively, through the whole service, to the precious word, although snow was falling. On Monday they had a meeting, and at the close asked the doctors and conjurors to abandon their deceptive work. They confessed before all the people that they knew that they could not help any one, and promised that they would give it up and burn their mysterious boxes at once.

One day an old chief came to ask a question. He said, " The white people are very wise ; they know a great deal, but the Indians are a very foolish people ;

they don't like what is good as the whites do. Why did not God make us all white, so that we would all be wise?" The old man seemed amazed as the missionary pointed him back to our common parents, to the origin of sin; and when he told him that it was Christianity that had raised the whites above his people, the chief said, " Take the door to every house; tell everybody about God."

Missions being established on the Naas, Rev. Mr. Greene felt called upon to make a canoe voyage up the Skeena. Calling his leading people together, he explained to them his wish to take the Gospel of Jesus to the distant tribes. They were well pleased. One said, " *Yes, there is food enough for all. Take them some.*" He writes:

"At Kish-pi-ax nearly four hundred people came to meet us as soon as they saw us, and made us feel how glad they were to see us at their village. They sat down, and we told them of Jesus and his power to save. Never did I see a people so eager for the bread of life. At the conclusion, after service, the chiefs spoke. One said, ' Your face makes me glad, and your words make my heart warm. I want God's word, and my people want it, but we have no one to teach us. We are glad you came to see us. You have walked five days across the mountains; now we know you love us. Put your coat down; stay with us, live with us; we want to love God. We will give up all the old way and do what you tell us. If you go away and leave us many moons, our hearts will get cold and weak.'

" Twenty miles more and we were at Kit-wan-gah, with four hundred and fifty souls hungry for the bread of life. After service they told me they wanted to be Christians; that half the village had thrown away the old dance and feast, and they wished to know when Sunday would come; they wanted to keep it holy, but did not know when it came, and had no one to tell them. It is quite exciting travelling this river. These gigantic mountains, the swift current, and 'shooting the rapids' fill every moment with interest.

"A young man very sick had his friends bring him twenty-five miles to the mission. He wept when he saw us, and said he wanted to hear about Jesus before he died. He said, 'I am very wicked; I want to get a new heart.' When we told him to pray, he replied, 'I can't; I don't know how.' We felt Jesus was very near as we pointed him to the 'Lamb of God.' When we called the next day he held out his hand, saying, 'Jesus has made heart good; now you pray for my wife.' He recovered from that time. A few days later his wife believed, and both are now happy in Jesus."

Unable to find an English missionary for these villages, Mr. Crosby stationed a native catechist at the forks of the river, central to the several villages.

At Kit-a-mart, one hundred and fifty miles south of Fort Simpson, a beginning has also been made, and a small church, twenty-eight by thirty feet, erected by the Indians. The lumber for this church was taken one hundred and fifty miles in canoes. The earnest desire of these Indians for light, and the exposures and hardships they are willing to undergo in order

A BELLA BELLA CHIEF. 323

to secure buildings for school and church, are something wonderful.

The most noted medicine-man of this place was Bella Bella Peter. He had been the leader of a secret religious society of man-eaters, who exhume dead bodies, bite and pretend to eat them. He was among the first to come to Christ. Bringing out all the implements of his sorcery, he burned them in the presence of his people. For a long time his life was in danger, his old associates fearing he would expose the secrets of their craft and deprive them of their gains and power over the people. But counting not his life dear, Peter continues to earnestly proclaim the truth as it is in Jesus, in season and out of season.

The people at Kit-a-mart belong to the Bella Bella tribe. And arrangements are made to station a Methodist minister at Bella Bella to visit all the villages of that people. At Bella Bella a little chapel has already been erected. Bella Bella Jim, one of the head chiefs of the nation, was a great gambler and drunkard. Being over at New Westminster he was invited to attend church. But he declined, saying he was not a church Indian. Again and again he was invited, until at length he concluded to go. He was so well pleased that he continued to attend. He concluded to give up gambling and drinking, and after a while saw himself a sinner and went to Jesus for salvation. After attending for a time the Indian church at New Westminster and Victoria he returned home. He had long been intending to erect a new house and make a great feast for all the neighboring tribes, that he might show his wealth and get great renown. But now all his plans were changed, and he concluded to build a church house that Jesus might get the renown. Thus was the Bella Bella chapel built. The church finished, he took his wife and child in a canoe and paddled two hundred miles to Fort Simpson, to beg that a minister might be sent to occupy the new house and teach him and his people about Jesus. He remained two months at Fort Simpson, under instruction in the new way.

The Hydahs, from Queen Charlotte's Island, have also again and again sought assistance and pleaded for a missionary. Hydah George, in the line of royal descent and heir-apparent to the head chief of his people, one night lay upon his bed of skins musing on the past. He remembered the ambition of his father and uncles for great renown among their people, but they had passed away. He thought of the desire of his sisters for wealth and display, to secure which they had gone into sin, which laid them in early graves. His proud family one after another had passed away until only he and a younger brother remained. The inherited wealth of generations had descended to him, and he was about to be made the chief of a powerful tribe. But as he remembered how only evil had come to his family, he determined to renounce the old ways of his people and try the Christian way. He and his people had often asked that a missionary might be sent to them, but none had come. He would wait no longer—he would arise and go where the missionary was. When he announced his purpose to his people, they were in a rage. They were afraid that the wealth of his family would be lost to the tribe, and they determined to prevent the carrying out of his resolution by force. He replied, "If it is my property you want, take it, but as for me, I am going where the Christians are." And the young man gave up his chieftainship, distributed much of his wealth, and taking his brother in the canoe with him came to Mr. Crosby for religious instruction. Thus from many tribes the people come to him for the Gospel. And his canoe voyages to visit them cover thousands of miles. I have dwelt more at length on these missions to show both the eagerness of the people for the Gospel and what can be accomplished. For what the Methodists and the Church of England can do for the natives in British Columbia can be done by the American churches in Alaska. They are the same people, with the same customs, practices, and heathenism.

Concerning them their missionaries write:

"The Indians of North America are so open to the Gospel that, from the experience of the past, the Christianizing of them is, with God's blessing, simply a matter of men and money. They are like fields white for the harvest.

"In the dioceses of Rupert's Land, where devoted missionaries of the Canada Missionary Society have for many years so lovingly labored, there has not been a mission where a clergyman has perseveringly worked in which the next generation has not become to a large extent Christian. There may be a trial of faith for a few years; then we perhaps hear—as lately in the mission at Fort Francis—of an Indian woman and her two children making open profession of Christianity and being baptized—first a few drops and then the shower. There seems no limit in Rupert's Land to the success God vouchsafes, but what we make ourselves. The people are everywhere prepared to anticipate, if not spiritual yet temporal blessings from the presence of a minister of Christ. There is a sense of the coming supremacy of the white man's religion. But, above all, the poor heathen Indian feels he worships he knows not what. He is conscious that if he speaks to his Great Spirit he is but speaking in the air. He hears no response. He stretches out his hand and grasps nothing. The future is all darkness. Where the heart feels such a blank, if not a craving, the way is very open to the sweet story of the Saviour's love."

REV. R. MACHRAY, D.D.

"The people have become convinced that the Lord is the true God, and many are beginning in simplicity and ignorance, yet with earnestness and faith, to pray for light, wisdom, and strength. Many an Indian has buried his old heart in the ground, and left there his old ways. From many a wigwam, where but a few short months ago charms were reverenced and demons invoked, ascend with unfailing regularity the songs and petitions of awakened men.

"Childish lips have learned to lisp 'Our Father

which art in heaven,' and adults to sing ' What a friend we have in Jesus.'

" The change has not in some cases been as deep as we could wish, but we can afford to be hopeful of those whose outward deportment has already undergone so material a change.'   REPORT.

" Cannibalism and cruel savagery have given way before the preaching of Christ, a Saviour suited to the Indians' deepest need. Souls has been saved and Christian churches formed."

" How they long for a missionary. They say,' How long before a missionary come? How long?' "

SLED.

www.ingramcontent.com/pod-product-compliance
Lightning Source LLC
Chambersburg PA
CBHW030011240426
43672CB00007B/909